Leopard

Animal
Series editor: Jonathan Burt

Leopard

Desmond Morris

REAKTION BOOKS

Published by
REAKTION BOOKS LTD
33 Great Sutton Street
London EC1V ODX, UK
www.reaktionbooks.co.uk

First published 2014
Copyright © Desmond Morris 2014

Printed and bound in China by 1010 Printing International Ltd

A catalogue record for this book is available from the British Library

ISBN 978 1 78023 279 9

Contents

Introduction

The leopard is the ultimate cat. It makes the lion and the tiger appear overblown and all the other members of the cat family look puny. The only exception to this is the jaguar which, speaking with an author's bias, I see as a counterfeit leopard that evolved in parallel in South America.

Lions hunt in the open and then share their kill but the leopard is solitary, stealthy and selfish. It ambushes its prey instead of chasing it and then carries its kill high into a tree where it can dine alone. In the wild, like Shakespeare's dragon, it is more feared than seen – a sinister, lethal presence lurking unnoticed in the undergrowth. If you are very lucky, you may just occasionally catch a glimpse of its athletic body lying limply and arrogantly along a convenient branch, resting in the midday heat.

The leopard is the feline killing machine in its purest form and, as such, has commanded respect and awe in mankind for many centuries. Jonathan Scott, the field-naturalist who knows more about the big cats of Africa than anyone else on the planet, has referred to the leopard simply as 'the perfect predator'.

In earlier days, when leopards were more likely to be viewed through the sights of a hunter's gun than through a naturalist's binoculars, their reputation was slightly different. Because they were so secretive and so good at hiding themselves away in the undergrowth, they upset the sporting gentlemen who were known as big game hunters. In the early part of the twentieth century, a certain Colonel Blashford was heard to exclaim, 'The tiger is a gentleman, but the leopard is a bounder.'

Since leopards are so stealthy, sighting one in the wild is a moment that one never forgets. My own moment came when, returning to Nairobi after a long filming trip in Kenya, my driver suddenly said 'leopard'. I shouted to him to stop and pushed my head through the open roof of the car. There, in a tree right at the side of the road, was an adult leopard nonchalantly sprawled along a high branch, it legs dangling lazily down on either side. I was able to take a photograph before being told that we had to move on as we had a plane to catch. It was a tantalizingly brief encounter, but it left an indelible memory and was the trigger that started my special interest in the species that has led to the writing of this book.

The leopard is a complex, intelligent animal and there have been dramatic incidents where it is clear that it is capable of bearing a grudge. One of the most extraordinary examples of its tendency to seek revenge when it has been maltreated occurred recently in Kenya. There, a female leopard had been preying on domestic livestock and the villagers had asked the local game rangers for help. Instead of killing the animal, they decided to catch her and transport her to a remote location, far away from human settlements, where they could release her. She was duly caught and placed in a travelling cage on the back of a truck. When they arrived at the release point, a game ranger opened the cage and quickly got inside the cab of his truck. To his annoyance, the leopard now looked upon her cage as a safe place and a snug den in which to stay curled up, and she refused to leave. In her stressed condition she was too alarmed to make a bolt for the wild environment outside.

After a while the game ranger lost his patience, leaned out of the cab door and began banging on the side of the cage with a

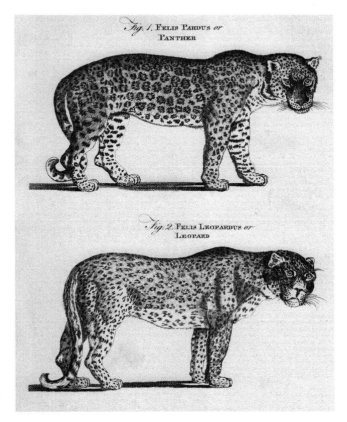

Fig. 1. Felis Pardus or Panther

Fig. 2. Felis Leopardus or Leopard

When the first edition of the *Encyclopaedia Britannica* appeared in 1771, the confusion between the panther and the leopard still existed, as is clear from this illustration.

heavy stick. The leopard snarled at him but still refused to budge. Then the man made a big mistake. He took a long, pointed stick and started jabbing the leopard through the wire of its cage. This made her roar and she grabbed the stick in her jaws and tried to wrestle it from the man. Eventually he gave up and sat back in his cab. At this point the leopard got up and walked out of the cage, but instead of running off into the undergrowth, as almost any

The author's first sighting of a wild leopard, resting in a tree in Kenya.

captive wild animal would have done in the circumstances, she prowled round to the cab of the truck and leapt through the half-open window. In his shock, the game ranger tried to wind the window up, but accidently turned the handle the wrong way, so that the glass was lowered instead of raised. The leopard was able to leap inside the cab, where she started to attack the man's head and chest, clawing him repeatedly.

This was not a cornered animal striking out in defence; this was a calculated assault. Pouring with blood, the game ranger had the presence of mind to push the leopard backwards with his boot and eventually to kick her out of the cab, whereupon she ran off. The man needed 21 stitches and was scarred for life.

This extraordinary sequence of events, captured on film, reveals the leopard as a thoughtful, vengeful being, capable of settling a personal score. I have observed chimpanzees, orang-utans and elephants behaving in this way, seeking retribution from those who have maltreated them, but I was surprised to find that leopards also belong to this elite club of the brainiest of animals.

This is probably why circus trainers refer to leopards as 'unreliable'. What they really mean is that, after suffering prolonged indignities, a trained leopard will one day decide that enough is enough and, without warning, take its bloody revenge. On the other hand, it is worth remembering that if a leopard is lovingly hand-reared with great kindness, it will grow up to become a loyal and friendly companion.

In writing this book, I will try to show all sides of the leopard's character – its athletic elegance, its predatory skill, its wary shyness, its cunning intelligence, its parental devotion and its preference for solitary living. I will also examine the many ways in which humanity has impinged on the leopard's world over the centuries – almost all of them to the animal's detriment. I would have preferred to tell how we have always admired and respected this great feline, but sadly I cannot. We have all too often hunted it, trapped it, slaughtered it, tortured it and generally exploited it. But things are changing and we are now, at last, starting to marvel at it and to conserve it. It is my hope that this book will aid this process.

Finally, a word about the name of the leopard. In the past, there was much confusion and even now there is some uncertainty. Centuries ago it was believed that the leopard was a cross between a lion and a pard, hence its title of leo-pard. Some authorities said that a pard was another name for a panther and others stated that a panther was a female leopard. The relationship between the pard, the panther and the leopard kept changing until, at last, the great Dr Johnson in his 1760 dictionary declared bluntly that a panther was a pard and that a pard was a leopard. In other words, the three animals were one and the same. After Johnson's time the pard faded into history, but the panther managed to survive, especially in the case of melanistic leopards which were usually called black panthers. Unfortunately, jaguars and pumas were sometimes also called panthers, so in the end it was the name 'leopard' that finally survived and became scientifically respectable. The leopard was, however, given the scientific name of *Panthera pardus*, allowing both its obsolete titles to live on in a Latinized form.

There was a second confusion and that concerned how many species of leopard there were in the cat family. The chart below, showing the modern classification, should clarify the situation:

LEOPARD (Africa and Asia)	*Panthera pardus*
AMERICAN LEOPARD (NOW JAGUAR) (South and Central America)	*Panthera onca*
SNOW LEOPARD (OR OUNCE) (Central Asia)	*Uncia uncia*
HUNTING LEOPARD (NOW CHEETAH) (Africa and Asia)	*Acinonyx jubatus*
CLOUDED LEOPARD (Asia)	*Neofelis nebulosa*
SUNDA CLOUDED LEOPARD (Sumatra and Borneo)	*Neofelis diardi*

Of these six, it is the first that is the subject of this book. For completeness, the other five will be discussed briefly in Appendix 2.

1 Ancient Leopards

The oldest known image of a leopard was found in 1994 in the Chauvet-Pont-d'Arc Cave in France. It is at least 23,000 years old and possibly much older. Although many other prehistoric cave paintings of animals had already been discovered in caves in France and Spain, this was the first example of an accurately drawn leopard, and it remains the only one. Like all Stone Age cave paintings, the animal's shape is reasonably accurate and there are no stylized exaggerations. The drawing may be very simple, but it catches well the proportions of an adult leopard.[1]

Careful studies of these animal depictions from the Palaeolithic period of European cave art have revealed that the animals are all portrayed in postures of death. In other words, they are memorials to individual, slain animals. The fact that they are of individual animals explains why they are so realistically presented – they are personal portraits rather than symbolic motifs. One of the rhino depictions in the Chauvet Cave shows blood spurting from the animal's mouth and it may be that the red smudge below the leopard's head is meant to show blood in the same way.

To find the next prehistoric representation of a leopard we have to move forward in time approximately 17,000 years, to the ancient settlement of Catal Huyuk in what is now modern Turkey. There, on one of the walls of a house, dating from about 6000 BC, is an extraordinary painted relief of a pair of life-sized leopards

Red ochre painting of a leopard from the Chauvet Cave in France, more than 23,000 years old.

shown head to head with their tails raised high. Nothing else like it is known from other prehistoric sites and we have no idea what it signifies, although there have been several imaginative suggestions. According to James Mellaart, who excavated the site, they are 'the attributes of the goddess'. This idea seems to be based on his discovery that, in a food storage pot, there was a statuette of a seated 'fat lady' flanked by two large felines whose tails curl round her back in a friendly way and hang over her shoulders. Those felines were not spotted but their small, rounded ears suggest that they too were meant to be leopards. The only alternative is that they were oversized domestic cats employed as pest controllers amongst the grain. This would make sense of the fact that they were placed inside a food container, as though they were put there to offer symbolic protection against rodents.

One thing is clear – the large pair of leopards on the wall had been there for a very long period. One of them had been damaged and this enabled Mellaart to examine its structure more closely. It emerged that, time after time, the figures had been replastered and repainted, as if freshening them up for a repeated ceremony of some kind. He estimated that they had been renovated about

40 times and made the memorable comment that 'at Catal Huyuk the leopard *always* changes his spots'.

The earliest images were considerably smaller than the surviving ones, had black claws and rosettes that were larger and fewer than in the later versions. At a later stage, the rows of black rosettes were painted on a white background, the bodies, legs and tails all being white. Two of the rosettes formed the eyes of the animals. Their mouths were red and their claws and the tips of the tails were all outlined in bright red pigment. Still later versions of the leopards were lemon-coloured and had black spots instead of rosettes. The mouths, the ends of the tails and the claws were now all accentuated by pink stripes. At this phase, the bodies of the animals were outlined with black dashes. Finally, in the last phase, the whole relief was crudely whitewashed and there were no details visible. By this time, the shapes of the animals had become clumsy from the repeated application of more and more layers of plaster. These outer layers were carefully removed by Mellaart to reveal one of the more interesting stages that lurked beneath the heavy surface.[2]

Further excavation at Catal Huyuk revealed that the leopard cult there had lasted for hundreds of years. Another pair of relief

Painted plaster relief of two leopards at Catal Huyuk, created about 6,000 years ago.

leopards was discovered at an older level, dating from about 200 years earlier, and a third pair was found at an even older phase, 200 years before that. In all three cases they are depicted head to head with their tails up. It has been suggested that this composition represents fighting leopards, but it might just as well indicate a friendly greeting between two animals. Alternatively, perhaps the correct interpretation is that they are meant to be dead leopards ceremonially posed as part of a celebration of the human conquest of a lethal feline predator.

Some small limestone carvings were also found at Catal Huyuk showing a human being sitting on a leopard's back. In these cases the leopard's spots are shown as drilled holes. Two of the figures sit sideways and one straddles the animal's back in the posture of a jockey. One of the damaged human figures is clearly female and one is shown wearing what appears to be a leopard-skin scarf. These figurines, probably worn as pendants, led Mellaart to describe the leopard as 'the sacred animal of the deities of the animal world and of nature'.

In a wall painting at Catal Huyuk dating from 5750 to 5790 BC there is a human figure holding a bow in its right hand that Mellaart has described as a hunter wearing a spotted leopard skin. If his interpretation is correct, then the occupants of this ancient settlement were not only creating effigies of leopards on their walls, but were also hunting them, killing them and wearing their skins.

It may seem surprising that leopards should be important subjects for the art found in a prehistoric settlement in what is now modern Turkey. Today, leopards are almost extinct in the Near East and we no longer associate them with the region, but 6,000 years ago these dangerous predators were common there and would have posed a serious threat to the local human population and, especially, to their domestic livestock. If the position

Clay figurine of a heavily pregnant female figure flanked by two large felines, found by James Mellaart at Catal Huyuk.

of the leopards in the wall reliefs suggests that, as with the earlier cave painting, they were being depicted dead rather than alive, then this is undoubtedly the condition in which the occupants of Catal Huyuk would have preferred to see them. This may give us some clue as to the nature of the rituals that appear to have been carried out over and over again.[3]

Moving on to the early civilizations, in ancient Mesopotamia in the fourth millennium BC there appears a remarkably lifelike limestone carving of a leopard. It is caught as if turning suddenly towards the viewer, alarmed and angry, its eyes staring, its jaws slightly open and its large canines clearly visible. It seems likely that the artist who made this figure had actually observed a leopard, perhaps one that had been trapped and was reacting defensively towards it captors. Its expression, its posture and its body proportions are all remarkably well recorded.[4]

A little later, in ancient Egypt, the long history of the leopard suffering for the beauty of its skin had begun in earnest. The high priests displayed their elevated status by wearing leopard-skin mantles – a costume accessory that must have been extremely rare and valuable in those days. We know from early records that

18

these skins were brought to Egypt from Nubia in the south as special tributes. One inscription includes the phrase: 'I bring it to thee from the land of the Negro . . . thy gazelles, thy panther-skins.' Their scarcity, combined with their beauty, not to mention the hazards involved in persuading wild leopards to relinquish them, must have made them greatly prized articles of ceremonial clothing.

There is an important tomb in Thebes that shows us in amazing detail what kinds of tributes were brought to Egypt and how these differed according to the land from which they came. On the wall opposite the entrance to the tomb there is a painting arranged row upon row, and from a copy that has been made of it we can see that the central row depicts the arrival of dark-skinned Nubians with their exotic, tropical offerings. These gifts include monkeys, baboons, a giraffe and a leopard. On the right there is also an impressive leopard skin, spread out for inspection. The walking leopard is being led on a collar and lead and is clearly a tame animal, probably destined for the pharaoh's private gardens

The tame leopard from 1500 BC, with its spots shown correctly as rosettes.

A bronze statue of the priest Anen, showing a leopard head attached to a star-covered skin. Anen served during the reign of Amenhotep III in the 14th century BC.

as an awe-inspiring pet. Despite its slim build, we know for certain that this is a leopard and not a cheetah because close examination of its spots reveal that they have been realistically rendered as leopard rosettes and not as the solid round spots typical of cheetahs.[5]

This painting comes from the tomb of Rekhmire the Vizier, the most important civil official in the land, whose job it was to check the pharaoh's gifts as they arrived. He served under the pharaohs Tuthmosis III and Amenophis II in the fifteenth century BC, at a time when Egypt's empire was at its most widespread and prosperous. It often happened that the pharaoh would keep some of the luxurious leopard skins for himself, either to be worn as dramatic capes or to cover the seats in his palace to make them more comfortable. Other skins would be given to favoured members of his court, to be worn on special occasions. It has been suggested that the spots on the leopard's coat had a special significance for the Egyptians because they reminded them of the stars in the sky. This idea is supported by the fact that when they made artificial leopard-skin adornments, they represented the spots as five-pointed stars.

The ancient Egyptians viewed the leopard as a sacred animal and as a personification of the sky goddess Mafdet. The link to the sky suggests the symbolic equation 'spots = stars'. There is evidence of this respect for the leopard as far back as the fifth dynasty, in the third millennium BC. One of Mafdet's sacred

Leopard skin displayed as a cloak, with head, tail, feet and claws still attached, worn by the Pharaoh Ay, successor to Tutankhamun, during a funeral rite in 1323 BC. The painting is from Tutankhamun's tomb.

duties, as a protector of the dead, was to attack the snakes and scorpions that would have hindered the journey to the afterlife.

Nothing is simple in Egyptian mythology and, in the case of the leopard, there is a completely different legend about the true nature of the big cat's famous spots. This concerns a struggle between Horus and Seth. Seth had the ability to transform himself into any creature when protecting himself from enemies. On one occasion he changed into a sandy-coloured leopard and his colouring enabled him to hide from Horus because it blended so closely with the desert sands. Horus, the falcon, circled high above, trying to spot his enemy in the desert below, but failed to do so. Anubis the jackal was more successful and managed to sniff out the almost invisible Seth with his sensitive canine nose. The crafty Anubis decided to make matters easier in future by branding the leopard to make him more conspicuous. Trotting over to the banks of the Nile, he paddled about until his paws were covered in the rich black mud of the great river. He then leapt on the back of the leopard and covered his coat in muddy paw prints. And that, the legend says, is how the leopard got its spots.

Compared with other sacred animals, it has to be admitted that the leopard does not seem to have inspired the ancient artists to any great degree. As the centuries passed, Mafdet lost ground to Sekhmet and Bastet, the deities associated with the lion and the domestic cat. There must be a thousand Sekhmets or Bastets for every Mafdet image in the arts of ancient Egypt. Of the few leopard models and sculptures that do survive, there is a small blue faience example in the British Museum and a larger, painted wood figure from the tomb of Tuthmosis III dating from the fifteenth century BC. The wooden figure is intriguing because it comes from the same period as the painted leopard in the tomb of Rekhmire the Vizier and has the same unusually slim build. It could be argued that these two images were based on the same, half-starved animal that was brought as an exotic gift from tropical Africa by the Nubians, but it is more likely that the slimness is simply a stylistic feature, because thinness in body shape of both humans and animals was generally favoured by Egyptian artists. An examination of the badly damaged surface of the wooden leopard seems to support this view because it suggests that the figure was originally painted black, implying that it was based on a melanistic leopard. Such an animal would undoubtedly have appealed to the pharaoh's court, being even more rare and exotic than the spotted leopards. Other details on this wooden figure indicate that it was originally part of a group and was probably accompanied by the striding figure of the pharaoh.

The tomb of Amenhotep II also contained a pair of black leopard statuettes that served as the base for a royal figure. In this instance, the proportions of the leopard's body were remarkably accurately portrayed, and the black surface has survived in a much better condition.

One curious object found in the tomb of Tutankhamun was an ebony folding stool covered in leopard skin. What was odd about it was that, despite its fold-up design, it could no longer be collapsed; also, the leopard-skin seat cover was not a real skin, but a highly stylized imitation of a skin, with the leopard's spots once again appearing as five-pointed stars. The strange feature of the imitation leopard skin on this stool is that the background is black ebony and the 'stars' or rosettes are inlays of white ivory. This reverses the natural contrast, where the rosettes appear as dark on light. If it were not for the legs and the tail hanging down, it would be hard to accept this as a leopard-skin stool. Sadly, the paws are missing because, it is believed, the claws were rendered in pure gold that was too good for robbers to overlook.

We are lucky that a number of gold leopard masks have somehow managed to survive the attention of robbers. These are

reminiscent of the belt buckles worn by some high-ranking officials. For the sake of accuracy, it has to be mentioned that, although these gold heads are always referred to as leopard masks, in reality they may be the heads of the hunting leopard, or cheetah. The clue is in the curving black line that descends from the inner corner of each eye. These lines are emphasized in the masks and, in nature, are found in the cheetah but not the leopard. The most impressive of these gold masks was found in a tomb alcove, along with the leopard-skin mantle of a Shem priest. The mask itself is made from a composite of rock crystal and wood, lined with pure, hand-beaten gold. In the centre of its forehead it bears the royal insignia – the cartouche of Tutankhamun. One of the nearby wall paintings shows the priest holding the mask in front of his face as he performs an important funeral ceremony. Bearing in mind the context of the gold mask, it is easy to see why it is always recorded as representing a leopard rather than a cheetah, and the true explanation may be that it was indeed intended to portray a leopard, but that the model enlisted by the mask's artist was a more friendly and amenable tame cheetah. Hence the cheetah's eye-lines on the sacred 'leopard mask'.

As Egyptian power waned and Greece became the new focal point of civilization, the role of the leopard changed. Now it became associated with the wild cult of the sensuous deity Dionysus. He was the god of wine and drunkenness, of chaotic sexual pleasure, of lavish partying and of ecstasy. Dionysus was depicted wearing leopard skins and even riding on the back of a leopard. So it was the wild carnality of the leopard that was being

Dionysus and his Leopard, 2nd century AD, mosaic.

25

The Tomb of
the Leopards
at the Etruscan
necropolis of
Tarquinia, Italy.

celebrated here, by the followers of this tempestuous cult.[6]
Dionysus can be characterized as the god of savage nature, of the
primal forces that lie outside the restraints of the civilized city,
and his companions the leopards epitomized this. They were also
said to have a passionate love of wine and to move with the
grace of one of his abandoned dancers. In one of the legends of
Dionysus, he is wandering the world when he is captured by
pirates. Two leopards – his sacred animals – appeared and herd
the pirates into the centre of their ship. Thinking they are going to
die, they all leap overboard but as they hit the water Dionysus
changes them into dolphins, so that they do not drown.

Leopards also make a dramatic appearance in the Etruscan
civilization that flourished from the ninth century BC in what is

now Tuscany, before the centre of power shifted to Rome. The Etruscans, who dominated Rome until the fourth century BC, created elaborately decorated burial chambers featuring scenes from the afterlife. One of these, dating from between 480 and 450 BC, is now known as the Tomb of the Leopards. It is in the necropolis of Tarquinia in Lazio and one of its wall paintings shows a great banquet taking place beneath a pair of confronted leopards. The big cats are said to be acting as the protectors of the revellers below them. They face one another with their long tongues sticking out and their jaws wide open. Also, each animal is depicted in a state of readiness, with one front leg slightly raised from the ground as if ready to make a strike, should one be needed. Their spots are clearly shown as rosettes, confirming that these are leopards and not cheetahs.

When the centre of power in the ancient world was eventually transferred to the Romans, the Greek Dionysus found himself transformed into the Roman Bacchus. Although he went through a transformation and changed his appearance, his faithful animal companions remained constant. In his new guise of Bacchus he could now be seen riding a leopard as a naked, drunken child, or feeding his sacred animals from a bowl as they reclined at his side.

This relaxed, symbolic presentation of the leopard would soon be overshadowed by a much more brutal role for the animal in the lives of the ancient Romans. The monstrosity that was the Coliseum was completed in AD 80 and its blood-soaked arena was soon to become the graveyard of many terrified leopards and countless other wild animals. The age of the persecuted circus leopard was about to begin.

2 Tribal Leopards

Leopards have frequently come into conflict with tribal societies, either because they compete with tribespeople as hunters, or because they prey on their domestic livestock, or because they occasionally become man-eaters. A large nocturnal predator like a leopard must always have been a threat to comparatively unprotected tribal communities. Viewed as dangerous animals, they therefore attracted two powerful responses: fear and respect. Fear of leopards led to rock art images showing the animal chasing running human figures. Respect for their strength and their cunning led to the wearing of leopard skins by tribal leaders who wished to absorb some of the predator's qualities.

The Bushmen of Africa were the original inhabitants of that vast continent until they were driven out by later waves of darker-skinned tribes. Today they only cling on in remote parts of southwest Africa, but their early rock art still survives all over the continent. It has been found as far north as the Sahara, and is a lasting testimony to their once enormous range. It has been estimated that there are probably tens of thousands of rock art sites in Africa, many of them still undiscovered. Some are believed to be at least 27,000 years old, but many remain undated. Many of these red ochre rock paintings by Bushmen show scenes in which their relations with wild animals are clearly depicted. Two scenes involving leopards reveal their fear of the animal. Unlike the prehistoric cave art image of a leopard in the Chauvet Cave in France, with its stiff, dead legs, these leopards are shown with angled limbs and are obviously running fast in pursuit of prey. The attacking leopards are shown closing in for the kill and one observer studying these paintings was prompted to remark that they were 'probably not self-portraits'.

Among the various tribal figures of leopards, the outstanding example, without question, is a pair of magnificent ivory carvings created in Benin in the nineteenth century. These were sent as a gift to Queen Victoria from Admiral Sir Harry Rawson who had been in charge of a British punitive expedition in 1897. The expedition of 1,200 men had been sent to Benin to exact revenge for the slaughter of a previous British force that had intruded there. The great City of Benin, one of the gems of African culture, was burned and looted. Palaces, religious buildings and the richest homes were torched. After three days of this destruction, the fire spread and engulfed most of the city. Its great works of art were either destroyed or dispersed, with 2,500 of them ending up in England. Queen Victoria, as was often the case when foreign

Bushmen rock painting showing a leopard.

Ivory leopards with copper spots from Benin, Nigeria, late 19th century.

looting took place, was the proud recipient of the greatest of the Benin artworks. The rest were auctioned off to pay for the expedition. Each of the Benin leopards is made from five separate pieces of ivory – comprising the head, the front legs, the body, the hind legs and the tail. The surface of the ivory, instead of being smooth, is worked into a fur-like finish and the leopard's spots are made from beaten copper. The copper is made from nineteenth-century percussion caps that were used for the detonation of rifles. The eyes are fashioned from fragments of mirrors that had been imported from Europe. These ivory leopards remain in the Royal Collection today but are on loan to the British Museum. All works of art in Benin City were originally made in honour of their king, or oba, and the leopard is recognized as one of his symbolic representations. Also in the British Museum is a smaller ivory and copper leopard from Benin, with a highly stylized head. This one was an arm ornament and was part of a ceremonial costume worn by the oba, who looked upon the leopard as the most powerful of animals. A Benin legend told how God had chosen the leopard for kingship over the other animals because of its great strength and beautiful skin, and its capacity to control an orderly, peaceful meeting of the animals.[1] As such, it was a suitable image to be used as an emblem of the Oba's authority.

One of the kings of Benin was so fascinated by leopards that he had special hunters sent out to catch live specimens for him. His captive leopards were revered as royal mascots and were proudly paraded on ceremonial occasions. There were times when he would treat them as an offering to his gods, but it was an established rule that only he was allowed to sacrifice one of these animals during the annual Igue festival.[2] This festival, which took place at the very end of the year, was celebrated to renew the king's magical powers and to allow him to bestow his blessing on the land and his people. The involvement of the royal leopards in this important festival shows clearly how central these animals were to Benin traditions. Their significance is underlined by the fact that a leopard was also sacrificed when a new king was installed. This was done as a symbolic demonstration that the new king (the ruler of the city) was taking over the power and wisdom of another king (the ruler of the forest).[3]

The casting of metal effigies of the leopard has an amazingly long history in West Africa. At the Nigerian town of Igbo-Ukwu, about 100 miles to the east of Benin City, one was found that could be dated as far back as the ninth century AD. It was an unusual composition, with the leopard standing on top of an elaborately decorated bronze conch shell. This dramatically pre-dates the famous bronze plaques of sixteenth-century Benin, meaning that, as bronze leopards are still being made in Nigeria today, this African tribal tradition has lasted for over a millennium.[4]

Benin bronze
plaque depicting
a leopard hunt,
c. 1500–1700.

Another extraordinary discovery at Igbo-Ukwu, dating from
the ninth or tenth century, was the rendering in bronze of
leopard skulls. It is known that tribal leaders sometimes kept the
actual skulls of leopards as symbols of power and aggression in
the shrines inside the men's meeting houses. It seems that these

Bronze plaque
depicting the Oba
of Benin sacrificing
leopards.

bronze versions, with their strange sculptural additions, were
also displayed in these shrines, probably acting as emblems of a
chieftain's high status. It is extremely rare for any tribal artist to
make a skeletal image of this kind, and it is rare, for that matter,
in any other kind of art before the modern age.

It may seem odd that the great king of Benin did not choose
the usually acknowledged king of the jungle – the mighty lion
– as his totemic animal, but the fact is that in African folklore
the leopard was the true king. It was only in Western eyes that

the lion was given top billing. There were several reasons why the African tribes preferred the leopard. First, they argued that although the leopard is smaller, it is more intelligent. Second, they believed that the leopard is a better hunter than the lion, and can kill certain large prey animals that even a whole pride of lions cannot overpower. Third, the tribal hunters found that it was easier to kill an adult lion than an adult leopard.

The rulers of Benin were so impressed by the leopard that they included special images of them among the famous bronze plaques that used to line their palace walls. One of these is now in the British Museum in London and it shows an elegantly streamlined leopard with impressive canine teeth and very large whiskers. Small bronze figurines of leopards were also popular and are still being made by African tribal artists at the present time. Some have exaggerated canine teeth, while others are shown carrying a cub in their jaws. They vary greatly in quality, from the skilfully elegant to the crudely cartoonish. In addition to these figurines,

Conch-shaped vase surmounted by a leopard, 19th century, from Igbo-Ukwu, eastern Nigeria.

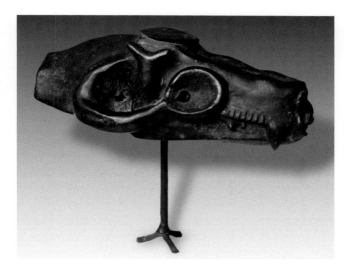

Bronze leopard skull from West Africa, 20th century.

there was also a tradition of creating expertly designed bronze leopard masks. Again, some had abnormally large fangs and whiskers. Several showed the animal with its tongue protruding, suggesting that the artist had copied the details of the head from a dead specimen.

Carving figures in wood has always been one of the most popular forms of art among African tribespeople. It is therefore surprising to find that wooden figures of African leopards are rather rare. When they do appear, it is interesting that, instead of emphasizing the leopard's predatory behaviour, they focus on its devoted maternal care, showing a female leopard carrying a young cub gently in her mouth.

Although as complete animal figurines leopards are un-common, there is one type of tribal carving that does favour them. This is the chieftain's stool that is a special feature of a number of tribes. With this important piece of ceremonial furniture,

Bronze leopard
mask from Nigeria.

Benin leopard
head-belt mask,
18th or 19th
century, ivory.

Ashanti bronze
leopard from
Ghana.

leopards are often included in the form of a support beneath the seat. It has been suggested that sitting on a leopard gave the tribal chief a sense of superiority over an animal renowned for its strength and agility. With a little luck, some of the animal's power would be magically absorbed by him when he was seated on such a stool. Among the West African Ashanti, where the leopard was said to be regarded as a potent symbol of tribal leadership, only the king was allowed to use a ceremonial leopard stool.

A similar symbolism is found among the Cameroon Grasslands people and in the Baule tribe of the Ivory Coast. As with the Ashanti, it was argued that the leopard's speed and aggression were attributes that were spirited onto the tribal leaders. The leopard therefore became an important royal symbol. As a way of increasing the visual impact of the royal leopard stool, it became the custom in Cameroon to decorate some of them with brightly coloured beads. One that belonged to the fon, or king of the Bali Kingdom, was presented by him to the British king, George v, as a special diplomatic gift in 1916, and it remains in the Royal Collection today. In one of the Cameroon Grasslands carvings, the tribal chieftain is shown sitting on the leopard, with a bowl balanced on top of his head. The leopard motif is so favoured that it is adapted to a variety of carved designs. In the case of the royal leopard stools, the king places himself on the seat above the leopard, but here it is the wooden, carved figure of the king who sits on the leopard. In both cases, the powerful leopard is subjugated to a position beneath the tribal ruler, giving him greatly heightened status.

African decorated cloth ornaments occasionally included a leopard in their design. These portrayals usually have a charmingly naïve, Sunday painter style that differs markedly from that seen in the much more assertive bronze figures and wood carvings.

Another way in which tribal leaders could absorb the power of the leopard was to kill one, skin it and use its pelt as a ceremonial decoration. The king of the Bandjun in the Cameroons has a leopard skin placed under his feet when he sits on his throne. It is said of him that he is the brother of powerful animals and that at night he is able to transform himself into a leopard and prowl in the forest. Hapi iv, the King of Bana, also in the Cameroons, prefers to have a leopard skin displayed vertically behind him when he sits on his throne. Alternatively, the leopard skin could be worn as a ceremonial robe. This was especially popular among the tribes of southern Africa, and with the Zulu people it remains so even today. In addition to a large leopard-skin shawl, many of these tribal leaders also wear leopard-skin headgear of some kind. Their proud and ancient custom is now colliding with modern South African attitudes towards animal welfare and conservation. Calls have been made that the leaders of the Zulu nation should publically reject the use of real leopard pelts and instead adopt

Ashanti leopard throne from Ghana.

38

Annang funeral cloth from Nigeria.

some kind of fake fur as their ceremonial costume. Experts in modern fabrics have been making special efforts to create an artificial leopard skin that is so realistic that it is impossible to tell the difference unless the material is closely examined. It seems unlikely that the colourful president of South Africa, Jacob Zuma, will listen to requests for these modern reforms. Instead, he seems to be revelling in a return to traditional Zulu values and is increasingly imitative of the Zulu monarchy – especially their leopard-skin attire. When he acquired a new wife recently, he celebrated defiantly in an old-style Zulu leopard costume, as did his bride.

The cultural link between the Zulus and the leopard is a strong one and it has a long history. In the early part of the nineteenth century, a great leader, Shaka, had arisen and amalgamated the Zulu tribes in a powerful warrior nation. As a young man, he had shown amazing bravery and had one day killed a leopard single-handed, using only two spears and a club. From this point onwards, the leopard had a special meaning to the Zulu people. It seems unlikely that a politically correct, counterfeit pelt will ever satisfy them. However, if wild leopard populations are reduced to a level where they become seriously endangered, they may have no choice.

Summing up the tribal role of the leopard, it is clear that, for the indigenous peoples of Africa, this big cat has been an important symbolic presence for centuries and one that has been given great respect. To many tribal societies, the clever leopard has always been more important than the mighty lion, and to all, it has been seen as a brilliant hunter that could be admired and even envied. The Yoruba reverence for the leopard was expressed in the form of a poem:

Gentle hunter
his tail plays on the ground
while he crushes the skull.
Beautiful death
who puts on a spotted robe
when he goes to his victim.
Playful killer
whose loving embrace splits the antelope's heart.[5]

3   Leopard Cults

Perhaps one reason why some people view leopards as unusually savage and cruel, when compared with the other big cats, is that for many years their name has been tarnished by association with the sadistic leopard cults of tribal Africa. These cults of murderous leopard-men have existed for centuries and are not, as some believe, confined to the pages of lurid fiction. They were active as early as the eighteenth century and were only stamped out by colonial governments in the middle of the twentieth. How many tortured and mutilated victims were despatched in their terrifying rituals during that long period it is hard to say, but the number must have been considerable.[1] Known as the Anioto, the leopard-men were members of a secret society who dressed in leopard skins and held sharp metal hooks in their hands with which they clawed their victims to death. The cult appears to have originated in the West African Mabudu tribe. From there it spread south to other tribes in the Ituri Forest region of the Congo. When they were performing their rituals, the leopard-men wore a real leopard's tail on a special belt that also carried a small pot, a carved stick and a sharp knife. They blew into the pot to make the sound of a roaring leopard. The stick was carved in the shape of a leopard's paw and they would use it to make fake leopard tracks around their kill. The knife was used to sever the victim's arteries.

In some areas, the leopard-men were little more than paid assassins who would target any village that displeased the local chief. In this way, they could help him to increase his hold on a region. Also, it was not difficult for them to spread fear that disrupted the daily lives of a neighbouring community and undermined the power of a rival chief. In other areas, the leopard cult was more concerned with superstitious beliefs and the conviction that by performing certain ceremonial acts the cultists could gain superhuman powers. Here, they not only killed like leopards, they also introduced elements of cannibalism. Each cult member had to drink the blood of a victim in the presence of other cult members and a special elixir, *borfima*, with supposed magical powers, was created from the victim's brewed intestines.

At their peak, the human-leopard murders became gruesomely extended killings involving increasingly elaborate rituals. In one region of Sierra Leone, the intended victim, usually a girl, was forced to walk in silence along a special track in the forest. On either side of the track, leopard-men were hidden in the undergrowth to prevent her escape. Then a terrifying growl would herald the sudden appearance of the particular leopard-man who had been chosen to perform the killing. Leaping in front of her, he would tear out her throat with a single strike of his metal claws. At this point, his hidden companions would gather round and carry her body deeper into the forest. There, they would decapitate her and remove her heart, liver and entrails. The rest of her body would then be carved up into pieces that would be wrapped in banana leaves. Each of the leopard-men would be given one of these pieces of flesh. Finally, her face would be cut away to disguise her identity.

Scenes like this were repeated, with local variations, many times in Sierra Leone and Nigeria, where the killings reached a peak in the early 1920s. Colonial administrators did their best to

The leopard-men in fiction, in a novel by Juba Kennerley published in 1951.

42

suppress the cult, but it simply went underground and was still active as late as the 1940s. It succeeded as a reign of terror because the local people believed that the leopard-men had the ability to shape-shift into real leopards and were virtually impossible to kill. Only when a determined local administrator set a trap using a human decoy, and shot the head leopard-man, did the cult start to lose its grip. The proof that the cult members were mortal and were no more than ordinary tribesmen dressed up in leopard masks and spotted clothing, rather than deadly, all-powerful supernatural beings, was enough to destroy their grip on tribal society. In 1948, cult leaders were rounded up and local chieftains were made to watch 39 of them being hanged in prison for their crimes. These chiefs then returned to their tribes and recounted what they had seen, finally putting to rest the mystique of the deadly leopard cult.

Tarzan confronts the leopard-men.

The fame of the cult had spread far and wide and in the 1930s the American author Edgar Rice Burroughs wrote a novel called *Tarzan and the Leopard Men* in which a fictionalized version of the cult was portrayed in some detail. With the typical racist undercurrent of the period, it was a visiting white girl who had to be saved from the clutches of the leopard-men by the heroic Tarzan.[2] Other books and films followed, and before long the leopard cult had become a cliché for any author penning a thriller about the savagery of the 'Dark Continent'.

4 Leopard Hunting

One of the threats faced by the wild leopard during the past few centuries has been the arrival in its territory of the great white hunter and the big game hunter. The pioneering explorers of the Victorian period would occasionally kill wildlife for food or to protect themselves, but the idea of killing large tropical animals purely for sport did not really gain momentum until the beginning of the twentieth century. Then, great safaris were organized to obtain trophies to hang on the walls back at home. No vehicles were involved; these were foot-safaris with a huge backup team. There were porters, tent attendants, askaris (armed guards), horse trainers, gun-bearers and a whole host of locals roped in for support. Some of the biggest safaris would employ several hundred African workers. When President Theodore Roosevelt went hunting in 1909, he took a support team of 250. His bag totalled 1,100 specimens, including 512 big game.[1] Despite the presence of teams of servants, there were many accidents. When it came to the moment of truth, it was the white hunters and their clients – adventurers, royalty, heads of state, film stars, international celebrities – who put themselves directly in harm's way. According to a history of white hunters, 'A staggering number of hunters died in pursuit of their quarry – mauled, eviscerated, or impaled on the tusks of furious, vengeful beasts.'[2]

Apart from President Roosevelt, famous figures who took part in these early safaris were Winston Churchill in 1908, King George V in 1911, the Prince of Wales in 1928 (before he became Edward VIII) and Ernest Hemingway in 1933. In later years, Hollywood stars who would glamorize these big game hunters included Gregory Peck (in *The Snows of Kilimanjaro*, 1952) and Clark Gable (in *Mogambo*, 1953).

At an early date, the colonial authorities discovered they could make money from these organized hunts. In 1909, for example, the British colonial government issued East African hunting licences for £50 – a considerable sum in those days. For this, you purchased the right to shoot the following: two buffalo, two hippo, one eland, 22 zebras, six oryx, four waterbuck, one greater kudu, four lesser kudu, ten topi, 26 hartebeest, 229 other antelope, 84 colobus monkeys and unlimited lions and leopards. The reason that any number of lions and leopards could be shot was that these big cats killed livestock and so were classified as vermin. At a slightly later date, the ultimate goal of the big game hunter in Africa was to bag what became known as The Big Five – elephant, rhino, buffalo, lion and leopard. Seeing these magnificent lords of the jungle crash to the ground was described as the most exciting adrenalin rush known to man. During the first half of the twentieth century, nobody saw anything unusual or cruel in these acts. No voices were raised in protest. In the cinema, the films showing big game hunters in action were full of praise for the bravery of the men and full of fear of the savage beasts that they confronted.

One man in particular helped to glamorize this new sport – the American author Ernest Hemingway. An avid hunter himself, he made the heroes of his novels men who set out to test themselves by stalking dangerous animals. They had to prove their masculinity by taking great physical risks and eventually killing

their quarry. In his stories 'Up in Michigan', 'Fathers and Sons', 'The Short Happy Life of Francis Macomber', 'A Day's Wait' and others, his male characters had to find themselves through slaughtering large animals. Famously, a leopard makes an iconic appearance at the start of his 1938 short story 'The Snows of Kilimanjaro', where, just before the start of the first chapter, there appears the following statement:

> Kilimanjaro is a snow covered mountain 19,710 feet [6,000 metres] high, and it is said to be the highest mountain in Africa. Its western summit is called by the Masai 'Nghe Nghe', the *House of God*. Close to the western summit there

Theodore Roosevelt with leopards he shot in Africa c. 1910.

is the dried and frozen carcass of a leopard. No one has explained what the leopard was seeking at that altitude.

Hemingway is obviously using this leopard as a symbol, but a symbol of precisely what is not clear. This point is still being debated and there are several completely contradictory interpretations. It seems probable that, in Hemingway's mind, this was an animal that climbed the great mountain in a desperate attempt to escape his hunter's gun, perishing in the attempt. Interestingly, his statement about the leopard's presence on Kilimanjaro is based on fact. There really was a frozen leopard high on the mountain. It was discovered in 1926 by the mountaineer Dr Donald Latham and was lying on the rim of the crater at a spot now known as Leopard Point. Latham cut off the leopard's ear as a memento and later climbers also took samples until eventually the leopard disappeared completely in the early 1930s. The missionary Eva Stuart-Watts, who climbed the mountain in 1929, offered a possible explanation of the leopard's presence in her book *Africa's Dome of Mystery:*

> Near the top we found in a perfect state of preservation the carcass of a leopard, first discovered in the snow and dug out in 1926 by Dr Latham of the Government Agricultural Department of Tanganyika. No one can tell what induced it to venture into a land so cold and desolate; but possibly the smell of meat carried by some safari had led it to follow their trail, until on the wild summit it perished in a snow-storm.[3]

It is sad that a man like Hemingway, who could write so well, was also cursed with such deep feelings of inadequacy that he (and his fictional heroes) had to spend their lives proving their

The famous frozen leopard on Mt Kilimanjaro, Kenya, 1926.

49

masculinity by slaughtering magnificent wild animals. And it is even sadder that, during the interwar period when he was writing, most people applauded his 'brave hunter' attitude.

It was not until the 1960s, when the conservation movement gathered momentum, that negative comments began to be heard. These arose for several reasons. First, in the 1950s, it was discovered that you could be even more courageous if you went stalking big game on foot armed only with a camera. If you shot with a camera instead of with a gun, you could bring back splendid photographs that were as good as the old-fashioned trophies. In some ways they were better because they provided a visual record of the moments of truth, when the unarmed 'hunter with a camera' came face to face with his quarry at close quarters. Second, documentary films were beginning to show a wide audience just how fascinating these wild animals were. The more you knew about their natural way of life, the more difficult it was to paint them as hateful monsters. Third, the early hunters had been so ruthless in their widespread slaughter that many of the biggest animals were becoming increasingly rare. Finally, to that can be added the dramatic increase in the human population of tropical Africa, which was doubling every twenty years, with urban centres replacing many of the tribal villages. Together, these factors changed the attitude of the public towards the big game hunter. He was now seen as an antique, a social fossil in the eyes of the modern world, a target for jokes, cartoons and comedy sketches. To the more extreme members of the animal rights movement, he was more than that – *he* was now the monster and had taken over this role from his wild quarry. The classic photograph of the brave hunter posing with a cradled rifle and with one foot planted on the carcass of his kill was now viewed as almost medieval in its barbarity.

Fortunately for Ernest Hemingway, he did not live to see this change, for in 1961, just as the backlash against his brave hunter philosophy was beginning, he took his favourite shotgun, loaded it, put the barrel into his mouth, pulled the trigger and blew his brains out. The hunter's torchbearer was gone and, with him, the whole era of 'it is manly to kill wild beasts'.

By the end of the twentieth century, the world of animal welfare believed that they had finally seen the last of those they labelled as 'morally bankrupt psychopaths'. But they were wrong. The fact is that the slaughter of wild animals by crack-shot hunters is still continuing today on a remarkably broad front. When America banned any trade in leopards or leopard parts in 1972 in an effort to stamp out the wearing of leopard-skin coats, a fashion that was threatening to exterminate wild leopards, they also automatically outlawed the importation of leopard-hunting trophies. The sport-hunting lobby began a long campaign to reverse this and in 1982 they succeeded in gaining official permission to import their leopard trophies, with the ban now being limited solely to commercial trade. Because they now face strong opposition from animal rights campaigners, the hunting fraternity makes less noise about its adventures than it used to, but the adventures still take place. And a book has been produced to educate young hunters in the fine art of leopard shooting. *CHUI! A Guide to Hunting the African Leopard*, by Lou Hallamore and Bruce Woods, was published by a company called Trophy Room Books in California in 1994 and reprinted as recently as 2011.[4]

There are about a dozen countries in tropical Africa that permit big game hunting in the twenty-first century. Each of these is given an annual quota by CITES (The Convention for Trade in Endangered Species), stipulating the maximum number of leopards that may be shot by sport-hunters in their region. In the following list, compiled for the year 2004, the national quotas appear in brackets:

Botswana (130), Central African Republic (40), Ethiopia (500), Gabon (5), Kenya (80), Malawi (50), Mozambique (60), Namibia (100), South Africa (75), Tanzania (500), Zambia (300) and Zimbabwe (500).

This gives a total of 2,340 leopards that may be shot for pleasure in tropical Africa in one year.[5] By 2011, seven years later, the figure had risen to 2,653, with Uganda and the Democratic Republic of Congo being added to the list, and with Namibia, South Africa and Mozambique doubling their quotas. The following excerpts from a statement by an African hunting organization explain the situation very clearly:

> Leopards are perhaps the most challenging of all the Big Five to hunt in Africa . . . The hunting of Leopards has become a controversial and sensitive matter, hence we can only hunt Leopard in certain areas in Africa and where the authorities issue legal permits and tags. In most countries the use of hunting hounds is not permitted, while others allow this. However, if you want a very memorable and rewarding hunt, then a fair chase Leopard hunt using bait and demanding all your hunting skills will be the most rewarding . . . it is important to enquire how many Leopards are harvested in a specific area annually, before making your decision . . . There seems to be a public outcry that Leopard are endangered throughout Africa. This may be true in some countries, or areas within countries, but this is not the case in others where Leopards are indeed often too many. All Leopard permits are issued by the Departments of Nature Conservation based on annual censuses . . .

One of the countries where leopard-hunting is condoned today is Namibia. The practice is defended by one of the Namibian hunt companies in the following way:

> Contrary to popular belief, Leopard are NOT endangered in Namibia. But because they are largely nocturnal and rarely seen, there is this wrong perception that they are rare ... Due to their secretive nature it would be very difficult to successfully hunt leopard on a 14 or 21-day safari without baiting. Baiting is the most popular method, lying in wait at dusk from a blind 75 or more yards away. Leopard are very alert, usually coming to the bait the last few minutes before complete darkness ... The real challenge is to pit your skill against that of the leopard, try to outwit him and get him to come to bait with enough light to afford a shot. It is said that you hunt an Elephant with your legs, a buffalo

Modern, licensed leopard hunters in Africa display their kill.

with your guts, and a Lion with your heart but a Leopard is hunted with your brain . . . Quick-expanding ammunition that will deliver sufficient hydrostatic shock will drop even the largest of Leopards . . . Namibia has of late become a very popular leopard-hunting destination.

One organization in Namibia quotes the following prices: 'Leopard Trophy: $10,000 to $12,000; Leopard Pre-Baiting: $2,500; Leopard Licence Fee: $1,000.' In Zimbabwe, one outfit boasts that 'due to excellent quota management we still produce monster leopard every season . . . the Bubye Valley Conservancy produced the biggest Leopard in Zimbabwe for the 2012 season, a monster tom . . .' They are offering a two-week hunt in 2014 for $15,400. In Mozambique, the cost is higher: '10-day Leopard hunt including 1 Leopard and Leopard dogs $29,500.'

It seems that despite the efforts of naturalists through their television documentaries, and animal activists through their energetic public campaigns, the ghost of Hemingway still strides out across the wild places of the world, intent on viewing a leopard through the telescopic sights of a high-powered rifle rather than through the long-distance lens of a modern camera.

This account of leopard hunting has focused on Africa. In India, the situation has been rather different. In earlier centuries the powerful maharajahs would mount great hunting expeditions, and although these were aimed principally at the mighty tiger, the leopard was also taken. Huge numbers of big cats were killed and their populations started to shrink. In Africa at this time, where there were only small tribal societies, there were no such onslaughts. When the great white hunters became active in Africa at the beginning of the twentieth century, the big cats were still plentiful. In India they were becoming less common, but there were still enough of them to satisfy the well-heeled hunters of the

British Raj period that ended in 1947.[6] In fact, major hunts were still being organized by the Indian nobility as late as the 1960s. When the Queen and Prince Philip were guests of the Maharajah of Jaipur in 1961, Philip took part in one of these hunts. The British press expressed outrage and an awkward diplomatic situation arose when the Prince was accorded the honour of shooting more big game on a second hunt. If he refused, he would be insulting his noble host, but the British press had reminded the British public that Prince Philip happened to be the head of the newly formed animal conservation movement, and that he was beginning to look completely hypocritical. (He served as UK president of the World Wildlife Fund from 1961 to 1982.) The imaginative solution to this dilemma was for him to develop a whitlow (an abscess) on his trigger finger that made it impossible for him to fire his hunting gun. So the killing of big game had to be done by other members of the royal party and he managed to avoid further criticism.

In 1972 the Wildlife Protection Act was introduced and the Indian leopard was placed on Schedule I (providing absolute protection, with offences carrying severe penalties). This meant that, from now on, even if a leopard was causing a problem, it could not be killed but had to be caught and relocated. This situation has persisted up to the present day. Poachers still take several hundred Indian leopards each year to sell their body parts in the Far East, but this is strictly illegal. So, although modern leopard-hunting is officially permitted in many African countries, in India it is a criminal activity.

Tigers remain the principle target of the poachers, but these are now so rare that the leopard is having to act as a substitute for its larger relative. According to the *Times of India*: 'The Central Bureau of Investigations' wildlife crime cell has estimated that for every tiger skin, there are at least seven leopard skins in the haul. In 2004, a seizure in Tibet of 31 tiger skins yielded 581 leopard skins.[7]

5 Leopard Attacks

Leopards have been killing and eating human beings ever since our species evolved. Even before we arrived on the scene there is evidence that, when our pre-human ancestors were living in southern Africa, they were prey to leopard attacks. The skull of a remote relative of ours, a juvenile *Australopithecine,* dating from 1.5 million years ago, had two puncture holes in it that perfectly match the canine bite of a leopard.[1] But once we had evolved into *Homo sapiens*, it is unlikely that we were ever a principle item in their diet. The reason is obvious enough – from a very early date our ancestors set up home in small settlements where leopards would be reluctant to intrude at night. If a small child wandered off into the undergrowth near a tribal village as dusk fell, it might be picked off by a leopard at the start of its nocturnal prowling, but such cases would always be rare. In those far-off days, human beings were thinly scattered on the planet and there was little competition for space. But as our species prospered and our numbers grew, the situation started to change. A serious problem eventually arose when human populations began to explode in certain regions. Tropical Asia was the worst affected. As India's teeming millions began to occupy more and more of that country, leopards found their territories being squashed closer and closer to expanding villages, towns and cities. Clashes were inevitable and the annual death rate started to rise.[2]

A drawing of the skull of a remote relative of ours, a juvenile *Australopithecine,* dating from 1.5 million years ago, with two puncture holes in it that perfectly match the canine bite of a leopard, whose jaw is here superimposed.

The first examples of this to attract widespread attention occurred in the late nineteenth and early twentieth centuries. Early field photographers brought the horror of leopard attacks to an international audience. One instance was the leopard of Gunsore in Central India. The Gunsore man-eater had killed and eaten at least ten people before it was gunned down by a British officer, W. A. Conduitt, on 21 April 1901. The leopard was killed on top of its final victim, a child from Somnapur village in the Seoni district of India. As the twentieth century dawned, the crack shots of the British Indian Army were soon in demand to come to the rescue of vulnerable villagers. One of the most famous of these was Colonel Jim Corbett, who was so successful at killing man-eaters that he was sometimes referred to as a *sadhu,* or saint, by the local people. His first success with man-eating leopards was in 1910, when he hunted down and shot the deadly Panar leopard that had reputedly killed and eaten as many as 400 people, but his greatest triumph was the killing of the dreaded man-eater of Rudraprayag, an adventure about which he wrote a best-selling book. This particular animal, a large male that had terrorized the local population for more than eight years, had reputedly killed and eaten more than 125 people. When Corbett finally managed to shoot it in 1926, he was hailed a hero. The extraordinary feature of this leopard's reign of terror was that it seemed to be fearless. In place of the usual shy, secretive approach of most leopards, this man-eater was a violent desperado. It was known to break down doors, leap through windows and even claw through mud walls to drag its victims out, carry them off and devour them. Nobody was safe. Repeated attempts to shoot it, trap it and poison it all failed. Eventually, Jim Corbett took up the challenge and undertook a concentrated, ten-week-long hunt for the now legendary animal. He began his campaign in the autumn of 1925 and finally shot his quarry in the spring of

The Gunsore man-eater after it was shot in 1901, on top of its last victim.

The Rudraprayag man-eater, shot by Col. Jim Corbett in 1926.

1926.[3] Today, there is a commemorative plaque at the spot where he killed it and each year a local fair is held to celebrate this famous event.

Leopard attacks still occur every year in India, but they are usually too sudden and too swift for any photographs to be taken. In a few rare instances, however, a camera has been present and the terror of the moment has been recorded. In one, a leopard that had already killed one man and injured another in a bold city attack in Guwahati, Assam, cornered a man in his bicycle shed and mauled him severely. The animal had been chased into the man's house by a panic-stricken mob in the city centre. What appears to be a dislodged hairpiece on top of the man's head is in reality something much worse – the leopard had scalped him with a single swipe of its razor-sharp claws. The leopard was retaliating after the man had prodded it with an iron rod in an attempt to persuade it to leave his home. The big cat was eventually shut in a house by a rickshaw driver, caught and taken to the nearby Assam State Zoo. The scalped man survived after receiving treatment in hospital, but a lawyer who was also attacked in his home during the leopard's rampage died of blood loss.

In the summer of 2011, a leopard strayed into the Indian village of Prakash Nagar. Surrounded by a crowd of onlookers, it panicked and injured six people before being tranquillized by forest guards. It later died in a veterinary hospital from wounds it had received at the hands of the villagers. In another 2011 incident, the drama of a leopard attack was caught on film at a village in West Bengal. An adult male that had been causing panic in the district was being pursued by forestry officials who were trying to drive the animal into a nearby wildlife sanctuary. Instead of fleeing the scene, the leopard, feeling itself cornered, went on the attack, leaping on the back of one of the foresters. Digging in with its claws, it attempted to deliver a killing bite to the neck, but the man fell off the wall on which he was standing and took the leopard with him. The animal then ran off and, by the time it was caught, it had injured six villagers, a policeman and four forest guards. It was subdued with a tranquillizer dart, with the idea of transporting it to a remote location for release, but it died

A leopard attacks a forestry official near a village in West Bengal.

within a few hours from the injuries it had sustained during its violent capture.

In the summer of 2012 an adult male leopard entered an oil company compound in the Indian village of Duliajan, having strayed from the nearby Joypore Forest Reserve. Once there, it attacked several staff members and an attempt by a security guard to net it failed. Officials from the Centre for Rehabilitation and Conservation of the Wildlife Trust of India were called in to help, but by the time they arrived, the animal had already injured five people. Veterinary staff shot it with a tranquillizer dart, but before the sedative could take effect, the now panic-stricken leopard lunged at what was by now a large crowd of onlookers. The security staff had no option but to shoot it, by which time it had injured a total of thirteen people.

A city attack by a hungry leopard in Guwahati, Assam.

The problem is also becoming serious in nearby Nepal. There, in 2012, one leopard turned man-eater. It had already killed and eaten fifteen people, including ten children. Its last victim was a four-year-old who was snatched from the family backyard. A search was organized in the nearby forest, but by the time they found the child, all that was left was the head. Explaining why this leopard had turned to devouring human flesh, a local ecologist suggested that it was because human blood is unusually salty and, once tasted, becomes irresistible. A more likely explanation is that once a leopard discovers how easy it is to kill a small human being, it overcomes its natural fear of entering human settlements and starts picking children off, one by one.

These tragic cases usually begin when leopards are attracted to the local livestock and village dogs. With their own natural prey becoming scarce due to encroachments into their forest homes, big cats are straying more and more into the outskirts of human habitation. Nocturnal filming in Indian cities has even revealed that adult leopards are commonly prowling the urban streets by night, knocking over dustbins and searching through house refuse for scraps to eat. The city worst affected is Mumbai. This is the fourth largest metropolis in the world with a human population of over 20 million. Amazingly, it also has the highest concentration of wild leopards to be found anywhere on earth. The main attraction for the big cats is the presence of the 150,000 stray dogs that roam the streets at night. London has now become accustomed to the presence of the urban fox. In Mumbai, it is the urban leopard.

Despite the increase in leopard attacks in India, as the human population has soared beyond a billion and the natural habitat of the big cat has continued to shrink, it remains a protected species in that country. When a specific problem arises, the normal strategy of wildlife officials has to be relocation. The leopard is trapped or darted and taken far away to a remote jungle location, where it is hoped that it will remain and revert to feeding on its natural prey. Sadly, this is a forlorn hope because the spot where it is released will already be occupied by other leopards who will drive the newcomer away. And, amazingly, leopards are capable of finding their way back to their original territories from a distance of as much as 300 miles, so they will soon set off for home and the whole cycle will begin again.

The disturbing truth we must face is that wild leopards and exploding human populations do not mix. As the naturalist Ron Whitaker put it in a recent television documentary, 'Across India two worlds are colliding. Every year scores of people are killed by leopards. And hundreds of these big cats are stoned, trapped or shot.'[4] 'How does one of the world's top predators survive in a country of over a billion people?', he asks. Not for long, is the objective answer. If the present rise in human numbers in India continues, there will soon be as many wild leopards in that country as there are wild wolves in their once native England.

Compared with India, Africa is relatively free of leopard attacks. On rare occasions an injured or sick leopard may attack a human being who gives the impression of being easy prey, but healthy leopards generally keep clear of human habitation. Even when curiosity drives them to investigate a building, the outcome is not always serious. There is an amusing story of a man who kept a pet leopard. One day, he found it in his room instead of chained up outside the back of the house where it should have been. He picked up a whip and drove it out of the back door, where he found his own leopard sitting chained up as usual.[5]

6 Symbolic Leopards

Because of their physical power, fierce temperament and beautiful coats, leopards have inevitably been exploited in many ways as emblems, badges, insignia, logos, trademarks, mascots, coats of arms and other symbolic representations. They have played a significant role in heraldry since at least the thirteenth century, and today no fewer than five African countries include leopards in the designs of their coat of arms: Benin, Gabon, Malawi, Somalia and the Democratic Republic of Congo. The identity of the leopards depicted in these five coats of arms cannot be in doubt, but in older heraldic devices there was some confusion between leopards and lions. This is because, in earlier times, the heraldic leopard was often shown without spots and sometimes even with a mane. What distinguished stylized lions from stylized leopards in those instances was not their anatomy but their posture. If the animal was shown rampant, it was a lion, but if it was shown walking, with its head turned towards you (a posture called *passant guardant*), it was a leopard. In England, this distinction was accepted until the end of the fourteenth century, when postural differences were ignored and leopards lost out to lions. 'The three leopards of England' then became 'The three lions of England', the now familiar emblem that every footballer is proud to wear on his shirt. Had there been any professional footballers during the reign of Henry III, they would have been proud to wear three leopards on their kit.

It was once believed that a leopard was a hybrid, or as a seventh-century authority put it, 'the leopard is the degenerate offspring of the adulterous mating of a lion (*leo*) and a pard'. As such, it was sometimes used in heraldry to indicate that the first bearer of a title had been a bastard. The arms of Richard the Lionheart were said to bear three golden leopards after the year 1195 because his grandfather, William the Conqueror, had been widely referred to as 'William the Bastard', having been the illegitimate son of Robert I, Duke of Normandy, by his mistress Herleva.

In 1992, the Republic of Tatarstan, part of the Russian Federation, adopted as its official state emblem a winged leopard with a raised right forepaw, bearing a shield and displaying seven feathers, seen against a sun disc. The winged leopard was chosen because in antiquity it was said to be a symbol of fertility and the patron of children. In their state emblem, the leopard becomes the

clockwise from top left:
The coat of arms of Somalia.

The coat of arms of the Democratic Republic of Congo.

The old heraldic leopard that became a heraldic lion, seen here in the Guyenne blason.

The coat of arms of Samarkand.

Two sports teams that employ the leopard logo: California's University of La Verne, and Pennsylvania's Lafayette Leopards.

Leyland Leopard bus emblem.

patron of the citizens of the republic, and its shield gives them security. The city of Samarkand in Uzbekistan has a very similar coat of arms, but in their case the winged leopard is *passant guardant* (looking straight at you) and there is a seven-pointed blue star in the sky.

Due to its speed, intelligence, athletic power and muscular strength, the leopard has proved a popular emblem among sporting teams. To give a few examples: the athletic teams of the University of La Verne in California are known as The Leopards; the South African Association Football team based in Limpopo are called The Black Leopards; the Lafayette University athletic teams have been known as The Leopards since 1927; The Atlanta Leopards female football team play in the National Women's Football Association in the United States; The Abaluhya Football Club in Nairobi, Kenya, known simply as AFC Leopards, is a professional football club founded in 1964; and The Dongguan New Century Leopards are a Chinese professional basketball team in the Chinese Basketball Association.

In the world of transport, the power of the leopard has led to its occasional use as an emblem, but it has always been

America's Black Panther Party logo, 1960s.

overshadowed by the ubiquitous jaguar emblem. The Jaguar car has become such an iconic global brand that to use a leopard in a similar context would always look like a feeble attempt at imitation. There were two exceptions, however: the Leyland Leopard, a popular single-decker bus, and the Nissan Leopard, a luxury sports car built by the Japanese car maker from 1980 until 1999.

A United Kingdom postage stamp with visual impact, 2011.

A more recent use of the leopard as a commercial brand was the 2007 launch by Apple of its operating system for Macintosh computers called Mac os x Leopard (version 10.5). According to Apple, Leopard contained over 300 enhancements more than its predecessor. Two years later it released a new version called Mac os x Snow Leopard (version 10.6). The aim of Snow Leopard was to surpass the already impressive Leopard system with a stronger performance, improved efficiency and greater stability. Its name was intended to signify its goal to be a refinement of the Leopard system.

The most famous of all leopard logos was not commercial but political. It was the emblem of the Black Panther Party for Self-Defense established in 1966 as the sharp end of the Black Power movement in the United States. As a black revolutionary social organization, it gained international notoriety for its extremist views. Allied to Marxist doctrines, the Black Panthers' avowed aims were to protect black neighbourhoods from police brutality. The savage power of the black panther in the party's logo, leaping at the onlooker with sharp claws extended, left no doubts about what the black activists wanted to do to their white oppressors.

In a more gentle sphere, the use of the leopard as a motif on postage stamps has been generally rather disappointing. In most instances, the animal has been painted rather inexpertly in a naturalistic manner, with insipid colouring and little visual impact. The exceptions to this rule have nearly always employed coloured photographs instead of paintings and concentrated on the head region of the animal.

7   Decorative Leopards

The beautiful coat of the leopard has been its undoing. It evolved as camouflage, allowing the animal to hide from its prey by breaking up the shape of its large body, but taken out of context its pattern switches dramatically from concealment to conspicuous display. As a result, the leopard's only serious predator – the human species – has persecuted it for centuries as a source of decorative clothing. Leopard-skin garments have been popular as high-status costumes across a wide social spectrum, from African tribal chiefs to Hollywood film stars, and from European queens to burlesque dancers. Anyone wishing to look powerful, exotic or wealthy has draped themselves in the undeniably attractive pelt of the unfortunate *Panthera pardus.* Nothing has threatened the leopard's survival in the wild more than this sartorial craving.

The first major assault on the wild leopard population as a source of spectacular skins occurred in southern Africa in the region dominated by the Zulu tribes. There, it was the custom for tribal chieftains to wear leopard-skin cloaks on ceremonial occasions. Today the practice continues, with members of South Africa's Shembe Baptist Church adopting the Zulu tradition and wearing leopard fur during religious celebrations. Even the president, Jacob Zuma, was recently seen to follow this fashion at one of his marriage ceremonies, despite being head of a country that has made the trade in leopard pelts illegal. Such is the irresistible appeal of the leopard-skin display. Jacob Zuma is not alone in adopting the ceremonial leopard-skin costume. Even the enlightened and saintly late Nelson Mandela was persuaded to adopt this form of dress on special occasions, as when the king of the Xhosa people awarded him an ancient tribal honour in 2004. It was the first time in two centuries that this particular honour had been awarded and Mandela was given the leopard skin as 'a symbol of the appreciation of his Xhosa people and of the African masses whom he relieved of the yoke of oppression and colonialism'.

For important rituals and ceremonies, a cheap imitation of leopard fur in not acceptable. It would be seen as an insult to the tribal or religious beliefs being celebrated, but Panthera conservationists are seeking to remedy this by creating fake fur that is so meticulously realistic that it is impossible, at a distance, to detect that it is not the real thing. They have been working with digital designers to create faux leopard skins that are accurate enough to be considered suitable for ceremonial use. If their strategy fails, the leopard will become extinct in southern Africa in a relatively short period. There are only a few thousand of

South Africa's President Jacob Zuma dressed for a marriage ceremony in 2012.

them left and the expanding Baptist Church now has over 5 million members.

In earlier times, when the British Army was active in Africa, some of the officers noticed that the local black African drummers were able to beat out a dramatic rhythm and co-opted the best of them for service with the military bands. Even as late as 1899, all the drummers in the military bands of the Royal Fusiliers were Africans. Later, when the black drummers had been replaced by home-grown white ones, the link with the African past was maintained in the form of ceremonial leopard skins for the bass drummers. Each drummer wore a complete skin, with a circular hole cut in the centre, so that the body and tail of the leopard were hanging down at the front and the animal's head region was on the man's back. This tradition was so ingrained that it persisted even into recent times, where it inevitably came into conflict with modern attitudes towards the wearing of real animal skins. When the Black Watch Regiment was embarking on a tour of America, they knew that u.s. Customs would confiscate any genuine leopard skins, so they took fake ones with them to avoid any trouble. From a distance these looked real enough but anyone taking a close look would have detected the subterfuge.

In Canada, the Calgary Highlanders, whose drummers had always worn real leopard skins, also decided to switch to something less controversial. In the late 1980s they adopted the North American black bear as the skin of choice. Black bears, being common, did not cause protests from conservationists and the regiment was able to obtain enough skins from road-kills to supply their needs.

Another instance of leopard-skin military adornment came from India, where the British Army and wild leopards were also both present. There, the leopard pelts were worn with great pride as part of an elaborate ceremonial uniform, and again it was the

Nelson Mandela in ceremonial dress.

Indian Army drummers in their leopard skins.

drummers who displayed them. The drummers have pointed out that there is a practical reason as well as a symbolic one for wearing these skins. They protect the drums from scratching by military uniform buttons and also protect the uniforms from the rubbing of the bass drums against the tunics. Of course, any leather apron would serve this function, so the specific use of the leopard is clearly also a way of announcing the savage power of the military wearers.

High society had yet to fall in love with the leopard skin as an article of exotic clothing. One of the first civilians to take the audacious step of wearing one in public was the rakish motor-car racing driver, William Brocaw. A photograph of him taken in 1904 on the occasion of the Vanderbilt Cup Race shows him sitting behind the wheel of his impressive vehicle, flamboyantly adorned in a leopard-fur coat. A commentator wrote of the occasion, 'The person who really stood out in this crowd was the "Man in the Leopard Coat".' It is said that the socialite playboy Brocaw was

William Brokaw
wearing
a dashing
leopard-skin
coat, c. 1904.

the real-life model for the fictional Great Gatsby. After this, it was not long before the boldest of fashionable women started to adopt this novel trend. In 1910, an advertisement for Knox Hats showed the wearer in a black-collared leopard-skin coat, and a few years later, in January 1914, just a few months before the outbreak of the First World War, the *Ladies' Home Journal* daringly chose a full-length leopard fur for its cover picture.

In the roaring Twenties, Hollywood discovered the leopard coat, and in the 1930s and '40s a number of female film stars were carefully posed for publicity photographs wearing this startling new costume, portrayed as the height of luxurious fashion. There was still no hint that it might be wrong to kill leopards to take their skins for luxury garments and nobody criticized these actresses for wearing animal skins. There were only two reactions – admiration and envy.

At this stage the damage to wildlife populations of leopards was not too serious. It was only the great divas of Hollywood who would dare to wear such exotic costumes. Polite society was still reluctant to 'go native' in this way. In the late 1930s, however, fashion magazines were beginning to hint at leopard furs as the latest thing in daring fashion for the wealthy and, had the Second World War not broken out in 1939, it is possible that the trend might have gained momentum. The war put paid to that and the post-war period was too austere to favour such blatant extravagances.

It was not until the 1960s that the leopard-fur craze really took off. This was a confident, boom period when displays of wealth were no longer viewed as bad taste. When powerful women began to stride out in exquisitely crafted leopard furs, the desire to own such garments spread like wildfire throughout fashionable society. In the early 1960s, the glamorous First Lady of the United States, Mrs Jacqueline Kennedy, the British monarch and the

queen of Hollywood, Elizabeth Taylor, were all pictured in this
exciting new style. However, it is doubtful whether they would
have worn these coats if they had known the impact their actions
would have on the wild populations of leopards. By the end of the
decade, a mass slaughter was under way to satisfy the demand.
In 1968, no fewer than 9,556 leopard skins were imported into the
United States alone. It took up to eight leopards to make one coat,
and soon the cats were becoming so rare that zoologists were

alarmed about the future of the species if the fashion continued for any length of time.

The craze had all begun when the New York designer Oleg Cassini suggested to Jackie Kennedy that she might like to be daring and try a leopard-fur coat, as this style had been out of fashion for some time. She was delighted and, as she was a style icon at the time, there was an immediate craze to imitate her. It has been estimated that the total number of wild leopards killed to satisfy this craze during the 1960s was something in the region of 250,000. When he realized what he had done, Cassini was horrified and set about producing a fake fur made from synthetic fibres which he hoped would be acceptable as a replacement.

Fortunately, it was in the 1960s that the modern conservation movement was set in motion, thanks largely to the efforts of the

Jackie Kennedy.

A young Queen Elizabeth II keeping warm in a leopard-skin coat on a chilly November day in 1952.

British artist and naturalist Peter Scott. This meant that pressure could be brought to bear on governments to control the killing. In 1969, the u.s. Congress introduced a conservation act that prohibited the importation of certain rare subspecies of leopards. This was well intentioned but it relied on customs officials being able to distinguish between the different races of leopards. As they were unable to do this, the trade continued unabated and it was not until 1973, when Congress introduced a more draconian conservation act that prohibited the importation of all leopard fur, that it was finally stopped. After that date, anyone in the United States selling real leopard garments faced fines of up to $100,000 and a possible prison sentence. In many other parts of the world the prohibition did not apply, but two factors helped to reduce the slaughter. Firstly, there were now so few leopards left in the wild that the cost of a pelt was astronomically high. Also, the new cultural mood of conserving nature made the wearing of any kind of fur coat less and less acceptable. There were incidents in which

Brassy barmaid
Bet Lynch of TV's
Coronation Street
in her leopard-skin
coat.

wealthy women venturing out in public in their furs were daubed with paint by angry activists and, before long, the fur coats of the world found themselves increasingly confined to their wardrobes. Every so often the fashion industry attempted to revive interest in them, but to little avail. In their place, fake fur and leopard-skin prints have become increasingly popular. The attractive spotted design has become a common fashion device in a more or less abstracted form, where it is abundantly clear that no animal died to produce it. Leopard-print scarves, dresses and swimsuits are still popular, although they have lost their glamour appeal and are now sometimes even looked upon as vulgar by the fashion world, because they are favoured by pop stars, actresses in soap operas and sex symbols. For many years, Julie Goodyear, in her soap-opera role as *Coronation Street*'s brassy barmaid Bet Lynch, displayed a strong weakness for leopard-spot designs and single-handedly managed to drag this motif so far downmarket that it appeared it might never recover. It seems somehow appropriate that, in her private life, she devotes much of her time to rescuing abandoned cats.

Even men have adopted this fashion motif. It would take a bold businessman to wear leopard spots to his office, but in the realm of show business, some of the more flamboyant personalities have been known to dress in this way when performing on stage. A famous example is the notorious rock star Iggy Pop, who became known for his leopard-head leather jacket in the 1970s. The savage, snarling face of the big cat on the back of his jacket went well with his group's album, *Raw Power*. Described as 'an iconic image that has gone down in Rock 'n' Roll history', this jacket was bought for $2,000 in 1998 by a collector who felt compelled to describe it as 'the Turin Shroud of Rock 'n' Roll'.

While these lowbrow displays were taking place, the world of high fashion averted its gaze. However, haute couture refused to give up the leopard pattern altogether because of its innate beauty. Even today it resurfaces from time to time, but never in the form of the real fur. The naturalist Christian Drake, commenting on its lasting appeal, believes that, 'We cannot shake the feeling that something, somehow led us astray from our true identity as the human ape, and adorning ourselves in leopard print reminds us of our species' connection to wildlife of the world and our once-intimate relationship to it.'

One decorative category where the spotted leopard pattern has failed to prosper is in the realm of female cosmetics. The reason for this is simple enough – make-up is meant to eliminate spots, not create them. As a result, leopard-style make-up is confined to exotic eccentricities and facial make-up with leopard spots is restricted almost entirely to children's fancy dress parties. The only place where the spotted pattern has enjoyed any cosmetic success at all is on the fingernails. Modern fingernail decoration has become increasingly elaborate in recent years, with fancy patterns often replacing plain colours, and leopard nails have enjoyed a minor success as a novelty item.

Haute couture
reclaims the
leopard pattern
in the 21st century.

Leopard-patterned
nail varnish.

A tattoo design
that displays
an anatomically
accurate, lifelike
image of the
leopard.

Leopards have enjoyed much greater success in the tattooist's parlour than they have in the beauty salon. In general, the most favoured motifs employed by tattooists are those that display images of love or of strength. The leopard's impressive muscular power appeals to many of those who are prepared to subject themselves to the pain of the tattooist's needle. The thighs, back and shoulders are the most popular locations for leopard tattoos, with the shoulder region being the most favoured of all. There are three basic variants – the lifelike head of the leopard, the animal's whole body or a close-up of a patch of its spotted fur. Anatomically, the head of the leopard is generally remarkably accurate, considering the medium in which the tattooist works. And the close-up fur patches create the uncanny sensation that the shoulder of the wearer is actually changing into part of a leopard's body, creating a strong desire to stroke the skin to find out what it feels like – which may be part of its appeal as a tattoo display. Tattooists who are asked for advice on having a leopard design done have a special patter to convince their customers that it is a good idea. The leopard, they say, is a symbol of strength, valour and power, and also of maternal gentleness. As a tattoo motif, they add, it makes an important statement about the wearer, because it signifies courage and personal leadership. Many succumb to the primeval appeal of this persuasive sales pitch. Although most leopard tattoos are on the limbs or torso, a few brave eccentrics focus on the extremities – the feet, the hands and even the head. Unlike the usually well-covered body tattoos, these leopard markings can only be hidden by wearing shoes, gloves, hats or scarves. The head examples, in particular, create a bizarre appearance that must make ordinary social life difficult.

One man who has taken leopard tattooing to the ultimate degree is Tom Woodbridge, who calls himself Tom Leppard and who lived a solitary life for over twenty years on the island of

Skye. There, despite the challenging Scottish climate, he could be seen scampering naked about the countryside, often on all fours, with almost his entire body covered in tattooed leopard markings. Inevitably, Tom is known as the Leopard Man, but he is not to be confused with the murderous African leopard-men who used to terrorize certain tribal societies. An ex-soldier, he abandoned human society after having his whole body surface covered in tattoos. The areas around his leopard spots are covered in golden tattoo paint and apart from a few crevices, such as the skin between his toes and inside his ears, every inch of him has been leopardized. Even his eyelids have been tattooed with designs of leopard eyes that stare at you when he closes his real eyes. He has also gone to the length of having his teeth modified with special implants to create a carnivorous snarl. It has been estimated that 99.2 per cent of his body surface has been covered

The tattooed Leopard Man of the Isle of Skye in western Scotland.

83

in designs, making him one of the most tattooed individuals in the world. Now in his seventies, he no longer lives rough, but still refuses to listen to the radio or participate in social activities of any kind. He not only looks like a leopard, but lives the solitary life of one as well.

Leaving the human body, many inanimate objects have also been covered in decorative leopard patterns, from chairs to shoes, bracelets to necklaces, and even cars. Among the smaller objects given the leopard treatment, there is one piece of jewellery of special note. This is a diamond bracelet that once graced the slender wrist of Wallis Simpson and was a gift to her from her husband, the Duke of Windsor, who gave up his throne as Edward VIII so that he could spend the rest of his life with her. This Cartier-designed bracelet, created in Paris in 1952 by the jeweller Jeanne Toussain, is covered with onyx and diamond and has

Leopard car at the 2012 Changzhou Automobile Exposition, China.

84

blazing emerald eyes. It was sold by Sotheby's in London in 2010 for £4.52 million, making it the most expensive bracelet in the world. The buyer remained anonymous, but it is rumoured that it was acquired by Madonna, who was making a movie biography of Wallis Simpson at the time. Another of Wallis Simpson's leopard jewellery items, considered by some to be even more beautiful that her famous bracelet, was a diamond and sapphire panthera pin, also made by Cartier, and given to her in 1949. It shows the leopard sitting astride a blue moon, the moon itself being a perfectly round cabochon star sapphire weighing 152 carats.

There have been many other leopard-inspired ornaments, of more modest value, from the exquisite to the tawdry. Many of the small leopard ceramics that adorn living room corners have bordered on the ugly, but a few have managed to catch something special and have done the great cat justice. One particular type of object that seems to attract the leopard image is, for some strange reason, the teapot. Some examples are simple shapes covered in the typical leopard rosettes, while others are more complex and may include modelled leopard elements that turn them into

collectors' curiosities. One in particular, fashioned in South
Africa and carrying an exceptionally high price tag, is deliberately
obscene, with the tea being poured through the animal's erect
penis. There is something charmingly perverse about making a
phallic leopard teapot, and it stands out from all the other leop-
ard-influenced knick-knacks as a minor work of art.

To most people in the West, the use of this spotted pattern is
simply a matter of employing a visually attractive decoration, but

The strange cult of leopard teapots. The connection between leopards and tea is not clear.

in the Far East it has had a deeper significance. It was believed that the use of the leopard motif, painted on a surface, could help to ward off evil spirits. In ancient China it was also believed that laying the head on a leopard pillow could protect the sleeper from nightmares because it kept the evil forces at bay. This may explain why it is possible, today, to purchase a complete leopard bed covering, including both pillows and bedspread. The only shortcoming with this form of bedroom decoration is that it looks so fearsome that it tends to ward off the sleeper as well.

One eccentric American house owner has gone further than applying a leopard pattern to a bedroom. At his home in the Rogers Park neighbourhood of Chicago, he has taken the unique step of decorating the whole of the outside of his building with a leopard design. There have apparently been no complaints, with other residents finding it strangely attractive. Despite this, it is not a house-painting style that has caught on.

Perhaps the strangest use of the leopard pattern is on coffins, a trend that has become popular since the late 1960s when it was

The leopard house in Rogers Park, Chicago.

88

Funeral service of a young mother, with her favourite leopard-print pattern.

favoured by the women of the Bohemian movement. There may be an echo here of the pattern as a protective device keeping evil spirits away and acting as a spiritual guard for the deceased in the grave. Some coffins are covered in animal leather but their symbolic impact is slightly reduced by the statement that, on these coffins, 'All leather is manufactured from cow hides and no exotic or endangered animal skins are used.'

In one case, there was a slightly different symbolism. After a young mother was tragically killed while attempting to save her children from a hit-and-run driver, she was buried in her favourite leopard-print pattern. In this instance the association with the leopard was through its fierce maternal devotion to its young and its speed of action.

8   Leopards in Art

Although a great favourite with the decorative arts, the leopard
has fared less well in the world of the fine arts. It appears far less
often than many of the other iconic animals, but there are certain
portrayals that are worthy of note.

MEDIEVAL BESTIARIES (TWELFTH AND THIRTEENTH CENTURIES)

The leopard makes a rather dramatic appearance in the bestiaries
of the twelfth century, where it is so little known that it is almost
a fantasy animal. It does sometimes have its famous spotted coat,
but occasionally this is lacking. It may have a mane, hooves, a sharp
pointed tongue, long horns, pointed ears or even a bright blue
coat, as it taxes the imagination of various bestiary-makers. Clearly,
nobody had told them about the ancient Roman mosaics that
were based on first-hand knowledge, and the Roman games
with their imported wildlife had vanished centuries ago. So all
the bestiary artists had to go on were a few wild rumours and
legends. One of these, curiously, concerned the leopard's breath,
which was said to be unusually pleasant:

> When a Panther has dined and is full up, it hides away in its
> own den and goes to sleep. After three days it wakes up again
> and emits a loud belch, and there comes a very sweet smell

from its mouth, like the smell of all-spice. When the other animals have heard the noise, they follow wherever it goes, because of the sweetness of this smell. But the Dragon only, hearing the sound, flees into the caves of the earth, being smitten with fear. There, unable to bear the smell, it becomes torpid and half asleep, and remains motionless, as if dead.[1]

Reading this, one could be forgiven for thinking that the panther of the twelfth-century bestiary had nothing to do with the true leopard, but was instead a completely imaginary, legendary creature like the dragon, but this is not the case. The bestiary author makes it clear that we are talking about the leopard when he gives the following description of the animal: 'The Panther is an animal with small spots daubed all over it, so that it can be distinguished by the circled dots upon the tawny and also by its black and white variegation.'[2]

The origin of the idea that the leopard has such sweet-smelling breath can be traced back to the work of Pliny the Elder. Writing in his *Natural History* in the first century AD, he says:

Panthers are light-coloured but have small spots like eyes. Their wonderful smell attracts all four-footed creatures, but the savagery of their heads frightens the creatures away. Therefore, to catch prey, panthers hide their heads as their smell attracts the prey animals within reach'.[3]

So the bestiary writers were not inventing the sweet breath, but simply copying it from a Roman author who should have known better.

When Pliny was writing, Rome was still importing wild leopards for the games, so he should have had first-hand experience of them, but the circumstances were probably against him. The wretched animals, severely stressed from their capture and transportation, must have been of little use as subjects for study, even if one could have got close to them. Probably the only information Pliny could have obtained would have come from the animal trappers who brought them to Rome. To succeed in catching lions, leopards and other wild animals in Africa, these men must have known something about the habits of the species they were seeking. They would have observed that, while other large predators chase their prey and run it down, the leopard hides in the undergrowth to ambush its victims. In other words, the leopard hides its face and lets animals come to it, rather than pursuing them. Pliny seems to have misinterpreted 'the animals come to it' as meaning that the prey animals were actually attracted to the leopard, instead of simply wandering close to where it was hiding. If they were actively attracted, then something had to be invented to explain the leopard's appeal. As the predator was invisible,

The sweet-smelling breath of the leopard attracted other animals, according to medieval bestiaries.

there could only be one possible explanation – it must have had an attractive smell. In Pliny's version, this invention is included to explain its method of catching prey, but by the time the bestiary writers had reworked his text, the predation had been omitted and all that was left was the leopard's sweet smell that attracts 'all the other animals except the dragon'. This is a long way from the truth, but it is at least possible to see how the fantasy leopard of the bestiaries grew out of the real ones in the wild.

In some of the early bestiaries, the leopard became symbolically transformed into Jesus Christ and the dragon into the Devil. The thinking went as follows: the leopard slept in its den for three days, then awoke and was followed by the other animals because of its sweet breath. This is interpreted as a parable of Christ rising from his tomb after three days and, because of his all-pervasive sweetness, drawing all mankind to him. Only the dragon feared him and, as the Devil, scurried away to hell.[4]

THE CLOISTERS APOCALYPSE (1300–1325)

Early in the fourteenth century, the leopard put in an extraordinary appearance in the Cloisters Apocalypse, transformed into a seven-headed monster. The verso of Folio 33 depicts three fantastic animals called the dragon, the beast and the false prophet. Unclean spirits emerge from their mouths in the shape of frogs. The reason that the beast is shown with a leopard's body is complicated. In Revelation 13: 2 there is a reference to the beast in the following words:

> And the beast which I saw was like unto a leopard, and his feet were as the feet of a bear, and his mouth as the mouth of a lion: and the dragon [Satan] gave him his power, and his seat, and great authority.

The Beast with seven heads from Revelation turns out to be a leopard, in a mid-13th-century Apocalypse.

The complex anatomy of the beast relates to its symbolism as a combination of the forces gathered against Christianity. The leopard element is thought to be traceable back to Alexander the Great's kingdom and the idea that Alexander conquered his empire with the incredible speed and killing ability of a leopard. Christianity wins in the end, when the leopard-beast is finally 'cast alive into a lake of fire burning with brimstone' (Revelation 19:20).

BERNARDO GOZZOLI (1421–1497)

In the *Journey of the Magi*, the Florentine artist Bernardo Gozzoli includes an interesting detail. He shows two spotted cats, one sitting on a horse behind its master and one on the ground, tightly held on a collar and lead by its sharp-spurred guardian. This second man has his left foot in a stirrup, as though he is in the act of mounting or dismounting. Gozzoli's attention to detail shows us that the two cats belong to different species because the one on the horse has the solid, round, black spots of the cheetah, while the one on the ground has the distinctive rosettes of the leopard. This detail is important because the slender body shape of the two cats suggests, at first glance, that they are both cheetahs. The implication of the rosettes is that both these species were being used for hunting, although this was usually the role of the cheetah.

Leashed leopard in a detail of Bernardo Gozzoli's *Journey of the Magi*, 1459.

JAN VAN DER STRAET (1523–1605)

Although born in Bruges, Jan van der Straet moved to Florence at an early age, where he became famous for his scenes of the hunt. These became so popular that they were made into prints and widely distributed. In two of his studies of the Roman games, he gives imaginative renderings of the trapping of wild leopards and of the moment that one of the captured animals has escaped from its cage in the arena of the Coliseum and is shot by the Roman Emperor Commodus, using a bow and arrow. There is no sympathy for the leopards in his work. They are depicted simply as savage, 'brute beasts'.

The trapping methods depicted by van der Straet show netting and trapping in a cage baited with a mirror. The latter is pure fiction. In reality, two methods were used – the net and the pit. Netting was the most popular method and involved men on horseback banging on their shields or holding blazing torches, driving the quarry down fenced alleyways and into netted corrals. The alternative was to dig a deep pit with a large central pillar on which bait in the form of a live goat or lamb would be placed. A raised fence around the pit helped to conceal it, so that when the predator leapt at the bait, it found itself descending into the pit below. A cage was then lowered into the pit to retrieve the captive animal.

PETER PAUL RUBENS (1577–1640)

In this overwrought, overblown composition, typical of the work of the Flemish artist Peter Paul Rubens, the leopard in the bottom right-hand corner has been killed by two javelins, one plunged into its belly, the other into its chest. It lies lifeless on the ground beneath the wild melee, its jaws sagging open and its tongue hanging out. This is a portrayal that sums up, in a single

Peter Paul Rubens,
Tiger, Lion and Leopard Hunt, 1616.

scene, the cruel stupidity of the popular attitude towards wildlife that existed in the seventeenth century. Artists like Rubens did untold harm by pandering to the coarser feelings of the people of his time.

In another major work by Rubens, *Peace and War*, or *Minerva protects Pax from Mars*, another leopard appears. It is alive this time, but as before it is relegated to a minor role, lying on its back as part of the entourage of the god Bacchus.

GERRIT VAN HONTHORST (1592–1656)

Although the seventeenth-century Dutch artist van Honthorst portrayed the leopard in a more kindly light, showing it quietly munching fruit while loosely held by a small Cupid figure, his sympathetic attitude to the animal is deceptive. It has to be remembered that the allegorical message of the painting is that, in this imaginary world of peacefulness and plenty, even

Gerrit van Honthorst, *An Allegory of Peace and Plenty*, 1629.

a monstrously savage brute such as a leopard will become soft and gentle and ignore the tasty parcels of young flesh all around it. So, symbolically, the leopard here is not a hero but a magically converted villain.

CARL BORROMAUS ANDREAS RUTHART (1630–1703)

Working a little later in the seventeenth century, the German animal artist Carl Ruthart reverted to depicting the leopard in its more traditional symbolic role as a bloodthirsty killer. Piling on the agony of the victim, he shows us a whole pride of leopards instead of a solitary killer. Whether this is due to ignorance, or simply a matter of artistic licence to intensify the brutality of the moment, it is hard to say. Also, instead of an antelope, the artist has shown the prey animal as a huge stag, a species that in reality lives too far north to be common fare for leopards. And instead of a herd of female deer in the background, he has chosen to include only a single hind, implying that the brave 'husband' is being torn apart in front of the eyes of his horrified 'wife'.

Carl Ruthart, *Leopards Attacking Deer in a Landscape.*

George Stubbs,
Sleeping Leopard,
1777.

GEORGE STUBBS (1724–1806)

George Stubbs, arguably the greatest animal painter of the eighteenth century, was primarily concerned with portraying domestic animals, especially horses, but did occasionally allow himself to indulge in the study of a wild animal, like this sleeping leopard, a small oval painting on enamel. Clearly based on a captive animal, it is hard to say whether this particular leopard is enjoying a relaxed doze after a good meal or has relapsed into a miserable sleep of enforced boredom, caused by being condemned to life in a small cage. But whichever is the case, this painting does at least sweep away all suggestions of savage brutality that were so common with earlier portrayals of big cats.

JACQUES-LAURENT AGASSE (1767–1849)

Jacques-Laurent Agasse was a Swiss artist who moved to London, where he became renowned as one of the best zoological painters of his day. He would spend a great deal of time looking at the caged wild animals in an exhibition that was open to the public in an arcade on the Strand. An important feature of his work was his sympathetic portrayal of these captive animals. These were not savage beasts, snarling and clawing the air; they were relaxed and almost friendly. It is true that the leopards in his painting might be rather bored by being forced to live in small, barren quarters, but they did at least have one another to play with, and that was how he chose to show them. This was a new way of

Jacques-Laurent Agasse, *Two Leopards Playing in the Exeter Exchange Menagerie, London,* 1808.

viewing potentially dangerous animals and it struck a chord with the Londoners of the early Victorian period, when a softer, more sentimental attitude to wild animals was slowly developing in English society.

EDWARD HICKS (1780–1849)

Edward Hicks was a remarkable nineteenth-century American folk artist with a Quaker vision of friendship and harmony that he expressed in varient forms of an oil painting showing prey animals and predators sitting down quietly together, *The Peaceable Kingdom*. In the bottom right-hand corner he shows a somewhat bemused leopard surrounded by a lamb, a goat, a calf, a pig, a cow and a small child.

Hicks became obsessed with this theme and did something that no other artist has ever done – he made 62 versions of the same composition, the first in 1820 and the last just before his death in 1849. The leopard is always there, but its position varies slightly from painting to painting. Sometimes it is sitting bolt upright, sometimes it is sleeping, sometimes it has a companion. In one of the last versions, dating from 1846–8, the title is given as *The Peaceable Kingdom with the Leopard of Serenity*, emphasizing the importance of this particular animal in the general composition. A catalogue describing the work comments: 'The spotted leopard, which serenely extends across the composition as though basking in a spotlight across a stage, was typical of Hicks' last years, representing a fusion of opposites that reveals the painter's inward longing for reconciliation.'[5]

A deeply religious man, Hicks based the scene depicted in these paintings on a passage from the Bible. Isaiah 11:6 makes the prediction that, at the coming of the Messiah, 'The leopard shall lie down with the kid . . . and a young child shall lead them.' So, in

these delightful allegories, we have an artist presenting us with a friendly leopard instead of one in the act of savagely attacking its prey or itself being savagely attacked.

Edward Hicks, *The Peaceable Kingdom with the Leopard of Serenity,* 1826.

ALEXANDRE CABANEL (1823–1889)

In nineteenth-century France, a highly romanticized Orientalism was widely popular. Cabanel's portrait of a pouting Cleopatra, lounging lazily with her unrestrained pet leopard, is typical of this genre. In the Victorian era, sentimentality about animals was beginning to replace brutality towards them, and this painting shows the animal in a much more generous light. It is still, however, cast in the role of a domesticated servant rather than a

Alexandre Cabanel, *Cleopatra Testing Poisons on Condemned Prisoners*, 1887.

wild animal in its own right. For true natural history portrayals of the big cats in their native habitats, one has to wait another hundred years.

JEAN-JOSEPH BENJAMIN CONSTANT (1845–1902)

Jean-Joseph Benjamin Constant's Romantic view of the exotic palaces and harems was inspired by a visit he made to Morocco when he was in his twenties. Many of his paintings showed half-naked odalisques reclining in palatial luxury and it was clear that these exceptional women would need careful protection from the outside world, hence his painting of a palace guard patrolling the grounds with a pair of adult leopards capable of tearing to pieces any unwanted male intruders.

J.-J. Benjamin
Constant
(1845–1902),
*Palace Guard
with two Leopards.*

JON HUNTER (1944–)

Now that the big cats are more revered and less persecuted, attitudes towards them as subjects for paintings have also changed.
In place of savage brutes being slaughtered, we now have more
sympathetic depictions of the animals in their native habitats. In
recent years, many natural history artists have produced accurate
portraits of wild leopards, but perhaps the most precise portrayal,
verging on photorealism, is *Il Gattopardo* by the contemporary
American artist, Jon Hunter.

Jon Hunter, *Il
Gattopardo,* 2010.

RAJABU CHIWAYA (1951–2004)

Modern painting from tropical Africa has often been disappointing but a remarkable leopard by the Tanzanian artist Rajabu Chiwaya of the Ngoni tribe is an exception. Chiwaya joined the Tinga Tinga Arts Co-operative in Dar es Salaam. He is one of the few artists in history who has used the leopard as a starting point for the creation of an imaginative animal image. Almost all artists who have depicted a leopard in their work have followed, to the best of their ability, the natural form of the animal, but Chiwaya joyfully plays with the image, creating a wonderfully bizarre creature in a scene that ranks among the best examples of naïve art anywhere in the world.

WALTON FORD (1960–)

One of the most extraordinary artists to have emerged in the United States in recent years is New York-born Walton Ford. His work has aptly been described as 'Audubon-on-Viagra'. At first glance, his watercolour of what appears to be a leopard applying a lethal throat-bite to a sacred, white, humped bull of India looks remarkably like an eighteenth- or nineteenth-century natural history illustration. Closer examination reveals that it is something else altogether. The first shock is the discovery that, far from being a book illustration, it is a work on paper that is 152.4 x 302.3 cm (5 ft high and 10 ft wide). Its meticulous execution may make it look like a traditional natural history painting, but in reality it is an allegorical work with a political message. The clue is in the title. *Chingado* is a Mexican obscenity that can be loosely translated as 'Screwed!' Because the bull is Indian, the feline is, rather naturally, referred to as a leopard. But it is not. Its flank markings show rosettes with small

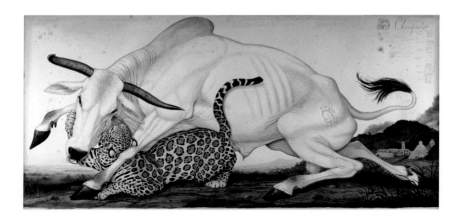

Walton Ford,
Chingado, 1998.

black spots inside them, clearly indicating that it is a jaguar. Also, the buildings in the far distance are pre-Columbian monuments. Despite the bull's white coat and humped anatomy, this is a Mexican allegory with what is intended to be a Spanish bull looming over an indigenous jaguar, who retaliates by attacking its assailant. In other words, this composition is symbolic of the Mexican peasants' struggle against foreign oppressors. A detail that is easily overlooked is that the bull is actually raping the jaguar, so the title applies equally to the throttled bull and the assaulted jaguar.

ZHANG DA BEI (C. 1970–)

Today, the leopard is a popular subject for young Chinese artists. One who has excelled at capturing the leopard's mood and appearance is Zhang Da Bei. Because of his calligraphic skill, he is also referred to as the master of Ximo Tang, but little is known about him since he has rejected all official approaches and refused an appointment as an academician, claiming to be 'indifferent to fame and wealth'. Despite this, he has been exhibited and collected internationally.

KUNA INDIAN ARTIST (20TH CENTURY)

The Kuna Indians living on small islands off the north coast of Panama will occasionally encounter a jaguar in the forest of the nearby mainland. When this happens, they will probably spot the animal resting on a high branch, and that is how they portray the big cat on the decorative panels worn by the women of the tribe. These panels are called *molas* and each woman has one stitched into the front of her blouse and one on the back. Those *molas* that depict jaguars reveal that the Kuna are not too familiar with this particular predator, its form being presented in a simplified,

A jaguar resting in a tree, as depicted by one of the Kuna Indian artists of Panama.

cartoon fashion. It does, however, display a spotted coat, a heavy body and sharp fangs and claws.

In summing up the ways in which artists have portrayed leopards over the centuries, it is clear that, although this species has never been one of the most favoured animal subjects, those pictures that we do have tell a powerful story of changing attitudes towards large predators. As the leopard's survival in the wild becomes more and more threatened, it seems likely that we will see increasingly sympathetic portraits in the future.

9   Circus Leopards

Leopards first appeared in circus performances in the days of ancient Rome. When they were released into the arena in those brutal displays, it was very likely to be their first and last performance because, in the staged hunts that were organized to amuse the jaded citizens of that great city, the animals nearly always ended up being slaughtered by the *Bestiarii*, or beasthunters. Some of the big cats were luckier and could avoid death if they could be taught to perform tricks. And others could survive for a while if they were employed in dealing with the criminals who had been sentenced to 'death by wild beasts'. The toll of animal life was staggering. During the opening celebrations of the Roman Coliseum, which lasted for 100 days, no fewer than 9,000 animals lost their lives in the name of entertainment. It is recorded that 410 of these were leopards. This mass slaughter of leopards continued for many years. Over 80 years later, in AD 169, for instance, we know that one event alone accounted for the deaths of 63 wild leopards. These staged hunts were not abolished until the sixth century, by which time it would have been hard to find surviving wild leopards anywhere in northern Africa or the Middle East.

Even at an earlier date they were hard enough to find. In a letter to Rome, written in 50 BC, Cicero complains about his difficulties when he is asked to supply more leopards for the

Leopard in a
mosaic from
a Roman house,
2nd century AD.

Roman mosaic
showing the killing
of a leopard in
the arena.

games. He was the governor of Cilicia at the time, in what is now southern Turkey, and he remarks:

> About the panthers, the usual hunters are doing their best on my instructions. But the creatures are in remarkably short supply . . . But the matter is receiving close attention, especially from Patiscus [who already had sent ten animals]. Whatever comes to hand will be yours, but what that amounts to I simply do not know.[1]

Trapping adult leopards cannot have been easy for the Romans who were living in the colonies in Asia Minor and North Africa. A third-century mosaic now housed in the Museum at Hippone in Algeria shows clearly how dangerous it was. Three leopards, a lion and a lioness are depicted in panic, corralled into a small space and surrounded, on one side by fourteen men equipped with large shields and savage prongs with flaming tips, and on the other by shrub-covered netting. A fifteenth shield-bearer has been thrown to the ground by the animals and one of the leopards is attacking his head. Horsemen on the right are driving the animals towards a box-like trap in the bottom left of the picture.[2]

At the end of the seventeenth century, Johann Graevius illustrated a leopard hunt in his encyclopaedic twelve-volume study of ancient Rome. Although many centuries have passed, the depiction of the trapping scene shows little improvement. Indeed, the portrayals of the leopards themselves are less accurate than those seen in the mosaic in Algeria.[3] It was not only the staged arena hunts that demanded the large-scale trapping of leopards and other wild animals. Some of the leading citizens in ancient Rome decided that it would be rewarding to have their own private menageries. The scale of these is beyond belief. It has been claimed that Emperor Octavius Augustus boasted a collection of 3,500 animals, including 680 lions and tigers and 600 African leopards and cheetahs. This obsession with controlling dangerous large animals was just part of the Romans' deep-seated desire to dominate the known world. When the Roman Empire went into decline, the wild predators were given a lengthy respite and were able to start increasing their numbers again.

Over a thousand years would pass before wild leopards would once again find themselves being trapped and dragged off to entertain a curious public. At first, they were exhibited in menageries and travelling shows when it was exciting enough simply to see them. It was not until the eighteenth century that a new era of circus displays, where animals had to perform for the public, began to appear in Europe and North America. Animal acts in circuses would now enjoy a 200-year run, from the 1770s to the 1970s, after which the animal rights movement caused them to decline and largely disappear in Western Europe and North America. In Eastern Europe, however, they are still popular, even today. Throughout this period, it has to be said, the use of trained leopards in modern circus performances has been extremely rare. In circus jargon they were referred to as 'unreliable' – easy enough to train but always prone to sudden, unprovoked attacks. These violent reactions were probably related to the fact that in the wild the leopard is not used to being in close proximity to other large animals, unless that animal happens to be a member of a prey species. It is as though the trained leopard is obediently following all its conditioned responses until something spooks it and, in a flash, it reverts to its natural, killing action of grab and bite. As a result, the more sociable lion has always been preferred to the solitary leopard as a performer in the close confinement of the circus cage. There have, however, been some notable exceptions to this rule and it is amazing to see the extent to which this secretive, retiring species has to be persuaded to modify its natural behaviour when displayed in the circus rings of the nineteenth and twentieth centuries.

The first important figure in this history of trained leopards was an extraordinary man called Isaac Van Amburgh. Born in 1808, at the age of 22 he startled his American audiences by entering a cage containing three leopards and three lions. 'The spectators were overwhelmed with wonder' when they saw these great predators draw back from him, as if afraid. As a finale, he instructed the animals to come to him and they obediently approached his casually reclining figure and peacefully surrounded him. His fame spread and in the 1830s he toured Europe for several years. When in England, he performed for Queen Victoria who was so enchanted that she commissioned Edwin Landseer to paint a portrait of Van Amburgh with his big cats. In the painting, which is now in the Royal Collection at

Edwin Landseer's portrait of Van Amburgh reclining among his wild animals, including two leopards, 1839.

Windsor Castle, one of the leopards is shown resting its head submissively on his thigh. The Queen was so taken by Van Amburgh's performance that she visited his show at Drury Lane six times and on one occasion even stayed afterwards to watch him feeding the animals. She would have been horrified if she had been told about his training methods. He relied entirely on cruelty to prevent his big cats from attacking him, beating them into submission with a crowbar during their training sessions. He defended his cruel treatment by quoting the Bible, saying that God had given him dominion over the animals. What is surprising is that none of his great felines attempted to take revenge on him for his brutalities. In a few seconds, any one of them could have put an end to him, but they failed to do so. Instead of suffering a savage death with massive feline jaws clamped firmly around his neck, Van Amburgh lived on to become a very rich man, eventually dying peacefully in his bed in 1865.

One of the earliest female circus trainers to attempt a leopard act was the exotic American performer Dolores Vallecita, born in 1877 and famous in her day both as an animal trainer and as a vaudeville star. Photographed in 1906 brandishing a whip at a snarling adult leopard, she manages to strike a dramatic pose only a few feet away from the animal's gaping mouth. Other performers who shared the bill with her referred to those times as 'nervous weeks'. Her act was popular all over the world, from London and Berlin to South Africa and Cuba, Egypt and Australia, but her greatest triumph was in India, perhaps because her big cats were all Indian leopards. Each of Vallecita's troupe of six leopards had its own personality. There was Grace the growler, a prima donna who would only work if she was given the largest of the travelling cages; Victoria the sly one, who always tried to gain an advantage over the others; and Tom the troublemaker who would stir up a squabble and then sit back and watch it unfold. Tom had killed a

keeper before joining the troupe, but this did not seem to worry the intrepid Vallecita. Despite their different personalities, all her leopards reacted as one if they saw a woman walking to her seat in the audience wearing a fur coat. Whatever routine they were engaged in, it came to an immediate halt and the eyes of all six leopards followed every move the woman made until she was sitting comfortably in the seat. Unintentionally, she had triggered their innate hunting response and, just for a fleeting moment, they were all wild predators again. Sensitive performers, they all shared a hatred of dogs, rustling sounds, loud bangs, spotlights, brass band music, jazz and the colour red. They all loved operatic music and Vallecita would play it to them to keep them calm between acts. This remarkable woman's career came to a sudden halt in 1925 when she rented the vacant Old City Hall at Bay City to train her six leopards. As she turned towards one of them, her favourite jumped on her, reputedly in an affectionate embrace, but one of its sharp claws severed her windpipe, her lungs filled with blood and she died. Despite the official claim that her death was accidental, it has to be said that when cats are affectionate, they usually keep their claws sheathed, so in reality it may have been a moment of jealousy when her favourite animal saw her paying too much attention to a rival.

Born a little later, in 1889, another famous female leopard trainer was the equally intrepid Mabel Stark, who started out her circus career riding lions. After she had been mauled three times she moved on to leopards and was mauled twice by them. She then switched to tiger wrestling. After that, she performed with a black leopard and was later mauled so badly that it was feared she would die. One leg was nearly severed, her face was lacerated, there was a hole in her shoulder and she suffered a torn deltoid muscle, but a few weeks later, swathed in bandages and walking with a cane, she was defiantly back in the circus ring once more. During the 60 years she spent doing her act, sometimes with as many as eighteen big cats in the ring with her at once, she was repeatedly mauled but refused to give up the adrenaline rush that by now she badly needed. In her autobiography, she wrote:

> The chute door opens as I crack my whip and shout, 'Let them come.' Out slink the big cats, snarling and roaring, leaping at each other or at me. It's a matchless thrill, and life without it is not worthwhile to me.

True to her word, when she was eventually fired by the circus, she committed suicide. She was 78.

A third remarkable woman, from a slightly later period, was British-born May Kovar. She was active as a leopard trainer in America in the 1940s. Her career came to an abrupt halt in a dramatic way. In December 1949, she was attempting to train a new recruit – a wild male lion – when the animal leapt at her and grabbed her by the throat, severing her spine. Astonishingly, May's teenage daughter and son, who were watching, rushed into the circus cage to rescue her, armed only with short poles. They started prodding the huge lion but it refused to release their mother's throat from its tightly clamped jaws. Luckily, an elephant trainer arrived and hit the lion hard enough to make it let go. He was then able to drag May Kovar from the enclosure and her children also managed to make their escape. But it was too late, May Kovar was already dead.

The classic shoulder-wrap pose with a trained leopard: May Kovar Junior in the 1970s.

The courage of the teenagers in attempting to save their mother's life in this way is beyond belief and it would seem certain that after such a traumatic experience they would never follow their mother into the circus. Yet that is precisely what the daughter did: May Kovar Junior became a successful big cat trainer in the 1970s, posing in exactly the same way as her mother, with an adult leopard wrapped around her neck. One may deplore the use of wild animals in circuses, but the bravery of the circus people themselves was truly extraordinary.

In addition to these intrepid women, there were several important male circus trainers who specialized in leopards. One who failed with this species was Terrell Jacobs, although it was not his fault. He was eminently successful with his lion act, during which he managed to assemble 52 lions in one enclosure. But the circus owner also wanted him to train a large troupe of black leopards that had been specially collected for the purpose in the steaming jungles of Malaya by the famous adventurer Frank Buck. Jacobs was only given three months to train these recently wild, caught leopards, which was a virtually impossible task. He failed and the act was never presented. Unfortunately, the circus had already arranged for the printing of a splendid poster showing all these black leopards performing, with the figure of Jacobs standing proudly in the middle of them. The posters were widely used, and the audience was often puzzled when Jacobs only appeared with his lions. His lion act was sufficiently impressive, however, to quell any serious complaints. And he did occasionally appear with a single black leopard that had been obtained from a separate source. Happily, rescue was on hand for the great circus because a Frenchman called Alfred Court was about to cross the Atlantic with a large group of fully trained leopards that would fill the gap left by Jacobs.

Alfred Court, a French acrobat from Marseilles, later a failed circus owner, turned his hand to training leopards in 1937. When his own circus had to be closed down, he gathered together an ambitiously large group of leopards and started to prepare them for an act he could rent out to other organizations. Altogether, he had fifteen big cats, including six spotted leopards, three black leopards, one Snow leopard, one jaguar and four pumas. With these, he toured Europe until the Second World War broke out, when he moved them all to America and joined the Ringling Bros. and Barnum & Bailey Circus, with great success.

Moving on to a later period, one of the most charismatic of all the circus performers who worked with leopards was the German Gunther Gebel-Williams. Learning his skills in Europe after the Second World War, he moved to the United States in 1968, where he became an overnight sensation because of the remarkable rapport he had with his animals. He replaced the old, bullying whip-and-stick approach with something much more friendly and respectful. It was his personal quest to eliminate the old-fashioned concept of 'man versus beast'. Gunther's vividly demonstrated love for his animals was much more in keeping with the cultural mood in the second half of the twentieth century and it was this that made him so popular. Over a period of 30 years, he performed live for a total 200 million people in a series of more than 12,000 performances and it is said that he never missed a single show. He made his last appearance in the ring in 1998 and died in 2001.

Historically, leopard trainers have used one of two techniques to develop their acts. These are called *en ferocité* and *en pelotage*. The first involved bullying the animals so that they were afraid to attack their trainer. There was a great deal of angry shouting and cracking of whips to keep the big cats in order. The trainer survived because he was feared. The second technique involved gaining their trust by petting the animals and rewarding them for learning their tricks. Early trainers used the first method and

The act that never
was. The famous
circus poster of
Terrell Jacobs and
his black leopards,
1938.

Alfred Court
launches himself in
America in 1940.

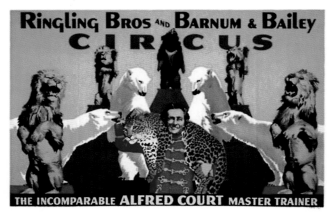

GUNTHER GEBEL-WILLIAMS
RINGLING BROS. and **BARNUM & BAILEY CIRCUS**
Produced by Irvin Feld and Kenneth Feld

The charismatic German circus performer, Gunther Gebel-Williams.

the more modern trainers opted for the second approach, even though it was more dangerous because it involved closer physical contact with the animals.

In recent years, investigations by animal rights activists have revealed cases of extreme cruelty by trainers that have led to demands for animal-free circuses of the type staged by the Cirque du Soleil. Britain will ban all wild animal acts in circuses from December 2015. Holland, Sweden, Austria, Greece, Costa Rica, Singapore and Bolivia are among the countries that have already imposed such a ban and many other countries, including Denmark, Finland, Switzerland and India and have already restricted the use of animals in entertainment. Clearly, an era is

May Kovar's performing leopards, 1971.

coming to an end, and although some countries still accept the existence of old-fashioned circuses, the days of the big top are numbered. Soon, leopard acts will become part of history. Animal programmes on television have shown these animals in their natural habitats and this has had a widespread educational effect that has made the public view with increasing distaste the artificiality of circus performances. They are increasingly aware that a travelling cage and a trainer's enclosure are not the proper places for a wild leopard to spend its life. But as these strange performances fade into the past, it is worth taking from them the memory of the leopard's unexpected flexibility and the remarkable way in which it was prepared to adapt to horrifically unnatural actions and postures. Looking at its life in the wild, one could never have guessed that this great predator would tolerate such impositions, but it did so to a remarkable degree and this lesson, at least, is something we can take from the traditional circuses of the past.

There is one other memory that should not be discarded with the spread of the new prohibitions and that is the bravery of the leopard trainers of the past. They may have exploited the animals and distorted their lives shamefully, but their own personal courage each time they entered the ring with adult leopards cannot be denied.

10 Tame Leopards

Tame leopards are comparatively rare. Tame lions have always been far more common, for two reasons. First, the bigger size of the lion and especially the huge mane of the male make it the more spectacular species to display as a close companion. Second, the lion is a social animal in the wild and therefore a more cooperative individual in captivity. The smaller and more solitary leopard must therefore be relegated to the B-list of Hollywood carnivores. But it has had its moments.

In 1922, the Hollywood star Betty Compson was photographed, along with her director, petting a tame leopard on the set of one of her films. A leopard wearing the same, sturdy restraining harness, and therefore probably the same animal, was also photographed at the Luna Park Zoo in Los Angeles in the 1920s, daintily feeding from a small bowl while lunching with three admiring women. When Hollywood wanted a tame animal for one of its films, it usually managed to find one and, from the early days of the cinema, there were always exceptional animal handlers on standby in Los Angeles to meet this demand.

In Howard Hawks's classic 1938 comedy *Bringing Up Baby*, the baby in question is a fully grown leopard called Nissa that had been trained by the Swedish animal handler Olga Celeste. Olga had performed daily with leopards at the Luna Park Zoo in Los Angeles for several years, and when a tame one was called for in

Katharine Hepburn in a scene from *Bringing up Baby*, 1938, with Nissa the leopard.

a movie script, it was Olga who was contacted to supply one. In the film, actress Katharine Hepburn is required to undertake a number of scenes where she is clearly at ease in close proximity to the leopard. She was known for her strength of character, but in these scenes it must have been severely tested. Cary Grant, her co-star, appears to have been far less happy about taking such risks. When he is onscreen with the leopard, some sort of movie trickery is usually employed, but this is not the case with Hepburn, especially in a scene where the animal rubs up against her leg in the manner of a friendly domestic cat. The leopard was encouraged to perform this action after Hepburn's dress was sprayed with a perfume that appealed to it. Hepburn's fearlessness was nearly her undoing. At one point, when she turned suddenly and her long dress swished out near the leopard, the big cat reacted by making a lunge at her back. Luckily Olga was on hand with a trainer's whip and was able to step in quickly enough to prevent any injury. During the course of filming, the intrepid

Hepburn enjoyed torturing the cowardly Grant and on one occasion caused him to flee in panic when she hid a stuffed leopard in his dressing room.

After the Second World War, Olga Celeste was still active and provided the leopard for the 1946 film *Tarzan and the Leopard Woman*, starring Johnny Weismuller. The plot of this film focuses on a secret leopard cult in which a high priestess – the Leopard Woman of the title – rips out the hearts of human victims as sacrifices for the cult's Leopard god. Tarzan demonstrates his knowledge of leopard behaviour when he sees a man who has been clawed to death. He is told this is the work of a leopard, but knowing that a real leopard would kill with a suffocating throat bite, he suspects foul play and utters the classic Tarzan phrase, 'Something leopard that is not leopard.'

In more recent times, a number of people have tamed leopards with varying degrees of success. Some have done it privately, but others have used the experience to write a book or make a documentary film. In 1968, Londoners were bemused, but surprisingly not alarmed, to see a young woman, Angela McWilliams, taking her pet leopard called Michael for a walk on a collar and lead along busy London streets. The leopard was calm and relaxed until she took it into one of the city parks, where it started lashing out at small dogs, who took an instant dislike to it. Her walk was filmed for British Pathé News, but there is no record of what happened to the animal.

In Africa in the 1950s and 1960s, while the couple Armand and Michaela Denis were making the popular television documentary series *On Safari*, Michaela befriended a young leopard and wrote a book about her experiences entitled *Leopard in my Lap*, published in 1956.[1]

In 1982, the Indian wildlife expert Arjan Singh became alarmed at the decline of leopard numbers in the region where he lived, near the border between India and Nepal, and he set out to see if he could return hand-reared leopards to the wild. To achieve this, he had to behave like a mother leopard towards them, walking with them through the jungle, encouraging them to hunt and even showing them how to disembowel their prey. Eventually, he was rewarded when one of his female cubs, then fully grown and living in the wild with her own cubs, was threatened by monsoon flooding. To Arjan Singh's astonishment, her response to this emergency was to carry her cubs back to his

Michaela Denis,
Leopard in my Lap,
1956.

house, one by one, and install them in a bedroom there. While the monsoon rain poured down, the mother leopard stayed in the house with her cubs and then, after about a week, she decided it was time to return to the jungle. She picked up one of her cubs in her mouth and set off, but found that the crossing over the nearby river was blocked by a large pool of water. Her solution to this was a vivid testimony to the remarkable intelligence of her species. She came back towards the house and then went to the edge of the river, where Arjan Singh kept his small boat, and jumped in. As Singh puts it, 'She could not have asked for a lift more plainly if she had requested one in words.' Singh started paddling her across, but the cub was too heavy for her to hold in her mouth for the whole crossing, and she kept putting it down in the boat and then picking it up again, each time risking dropping it overboard. Once they reached the other bank, she took the cub firmly in her mouth, jumped out of the boat and disappeared. Singh waited for her, but she was away so long that he rowed back. No sooner had he done this, than there she was, on the other bank, calling to him to return for her. Describing himself as a well-trained gondolier, he set off once again, collected her and brought her back. She went into the house, collected her second cub and jumped into her ferry for a final crossing. Some weeks later, when Singh went into the jungle to look for her, she was prepared to show him her cubs, now grown much bigger and stronger. This is an extraordinary incident and it is hard to imagine any other species being adaptable enough to take her wild-born cubs into a house to protect them from flooding and then demanding human assistance to take them back to the jungle in a boat when the flooding had subsided. Were it not for a photograph of the event, one could be forgiven for thinking it was a tall story.[2]

In recent years, several specialist companies have been established in the United States and Europe to supply exotic animals for appearances on television, film and advertising work. These companies are staffed by experts who sometimes achieve remarkable relationships with dangerous animals. Whether wild animals should be exploited in this way remains a matter of debate, but what these companies demonstrate is that, with expert handling, even an adult leopard can be made tame enough to perform for the camera. They teach us the valuable lesson that, when trained by reward rather than punishment, the traditional labelling of the leopard as an 'unreliable' species is unfounded.

Perhaps the most extraordinary relationship between a free-living leopard and a human being is the one that existed between an adult leopard and a tiny French girl called Tippi who was living with her parents, Sylvie Robert and Alain Degré, in Namibia in southwest Africa. Tippi was born and raised surrounded by wild animals and treated them as her friends. Other small children are given soft animal toys to play with, but Tippi enjoyed the real thing and her natural, relaxed behaviour around them made them trust her and treat her as one of them. Tippi's parents were wildlife photographers and they made a detailed record of the small girl's life as she grew up in what, for her, was a tropical paradise. Amazingly, she survived all her animal adventures unscathed and later could be found in a very different setting – Paris, aged eighteen, studying for a degree at the Sorbonne. Her parents' book *Tippi: My Book of Africa* was published to tell her remarkable story.[3]

11 Wild Leopards

Up to this point, the leopard has been viewed in its many different interactions with mankind. Ancients have revered it, gladiators have slaughtered it, leopard-men have imitated it, big game hunters have shot it, villagers have feared it, celebrities have worn it, artists have portrayed it, circus performers have trained it and a brave few have tamed it. But what do we know about its natural history, about the animal itself?

The first animal encyclopaedia to be published in English was Edward Topsell's 1658 *The History of Four-footed Beasts* in which he devotes nine pages to the leopard. It is clear that, at this point, there was scant knowledge of the true nature of the species. Topsell fills his pages with bizarre facts, such as the recommendation that the brains of leopards, when mixed with jasmine, are a useful cure for bellyache. As regards the animal's disposition, he tells his readers that it is 'wanton, effeminate, outrageous, treacherous, deceitful, fearful and yet bold'.[1] But what is the true story of the leopard, as it lives its life in the wild? It is such a secretive, elusive animal that, until recently, the precise details of its natural behaviour were largely unknown. Early fieldworkers found it easier to study the prides of lions that were bold enough to display themselves brashly in open country. Leopards were occasionally seen sleeping on high branches during the heat of the day, and were heard calling at night, but beyond that they were almost invisible.

This invisibility is, of course, the secret of their success. It is their cautious temperament, combined with a remarkable flexibility in their choice of habitat and prey, that has made them the most widespread of all the big cats. Even the lion's vast geographical range cannot compete with theirs. Historically, leopards have been found throughout Africa, the Middle East and in Asia, from the tropical south to the frozen north. The relentless hunting for their beautiful skins and the enormous increase in human populations have, inevitably, reduced their numbers in many areas, but their secretive lifestyle has served them well in their struggle to survive. Their numbers may have shrunk, but their geographical range is still the largest of any of the big cats.

One unusual feature of the leopard's behaviour in the wild concerns its diet. It is true to say that it is the only member of the cat family to hunt, kill and eat both very large and very small prey on a regular basis. There is a popular generalization that says that the big cats (genus *Panthera*) eat large animals, while the lesser cats (genus *Felis*) eat small animals. There is some truth in this – big cats prefer antelope and small cats prefer rodents – but there are many exceptions, and the biggest exception of all is to be found in the menu of the leopard. It will attack and devour

The anatomy of the leopard according to Topsell in 1658.

everything from large antelopes to gazelles, warthogs, apes, monkeys, pythons, mongooses, foxes, jackals, hares, storks, small birds and rats. This readiness to switch from one kind of diet to another is part of the reason why it has been able to succeed in so many different habitats.

When hunting for birds, a leopard will hide near a watering hole in the early morning and, when a flock of well-watered sand-grouse, or similar birds, flies away, it will leap vertically in the air, snatch out with its sharp, curved claws and catch an unsuspecting bird in flight. One environmental feature it will always seek, however, is cover. In particular, it craves three things: a tall tree in which to rest, a rocky crevice in which to rear its cubs and thick undergrowth in which to hide. Given these, it will live almost anywhere, from the steaming tropical forests, to the edges of deserts and the frozen mountains of Russia.

Leopards vary in size quite considerably. The smallest adult, from nose to tail tip, would be about 170 cm (5.5 ft) long; the largest as much as 280 cm (9 ft). Males are bigger than females and the cold-country leopards bigger than the hot-country ones. They weigh between 30 and 70 kg (65 and 160 lb) and have an average life-span in the wild of only about twelve years, but this can be stretched to as long as twenty years if pampered in captivity. One of the reasons why the leopard is smaller than the lion or the tiger is that its more modest size enables it to out-climb its big cat rivals. During its evolution, it grew as big and as powerful as possible, without exceeding the weight that would permit its rapid ascent into the high branches. Amazingly, it can carry a freshly killed prey animal that weighs more than itself up into a safe place in the trees. The smell of its kill often attracts a passing lion and the lion may even begin climbing upwards in an attempt to steal the carcass, but it rarely manages to reach it. High up, the leopard can rest, sleep and eat at leisure. One leopard was even

Leopards feel secure in the high branches during the day.

The camouflage markings on the leopard's coat help to break up the shape of its body.

seen to have three dead gazelles draped on the branches of a single tree – a bulging larder awaiting the predator's pleasure.

With larger prey, the leopard will disembowel its kill and bury the entrails before it starts to feed. If it is in a region where there is no threat from earthbound rivals, it will not go to the trouble of carrying the carcass up into a tree, but will devour it on the ground. If it has eaten its fill and there is meat left over, it will cover the remains with soil, leaves and branches and then return to it at a later time. If there is the slightest sign of danger, however, it grabs the freshly killed prey by the neck and clambers aloft with it. Having to keep its body weight down to a level that permits arboreal retreat does, however, create a problem at ground level. Face to face with a lion or a pack of hungry hyenas, the leopard is a poor opponent, and it will think twice about challenging a troop of baboons, whose sturdy males are capable of

An African leopard attacking a baboon.

ganging up to create a formidable defensive team. It will even abandon a fresh kill which it has not yet managed to heave up into a tree if approached by rival predators.

The leopard's survival strategy is always to play it safe. This is why it has been called 'the invisible cat'. At ground level it is a shadowy, lurking presence, forever skulking off, crouching and hiding. It is so seldom seen that people living in tropical cities are often unaware that there are leopards prowling their streets at night, hunting stray dogs, cats and sewer rats. At the first sign of trouble, these wary hunters dissolve into the night.

So the mighty leopard is, in reality, a cunning mixture of camouflage, patience, caution, adaptability, curiosity and athleticism. Given this combination, it is not surprising that Jonathan Scott christened it 'the perfect predator'.

Another notable feature of the wild leopard is that it is one of the most solitary of all felines. Each leopard has a large home range, from 3 square miles up to as much as 30 square miles in size. There may be a small degree of overlapping with other individual leopards, but careful scent-marking and scratch-marking ensure that they hardly ever meet. They regularly patrol

A leopard catching a sandgrouse in mid-air near a water hole in the Kgalagadi Transfrontier Park, on the borders between Botswana and South Africa.

their territories, checking for any recent scents or scratch marks, the close examination of which will tell them a great deal about their neighbours. But instead of leading to confrontations, this marking behaviour ensures that they can avoid one another. The social life of the leopard is restricted to brief mating encounters and to prolonged periods of maternal care of cubs. The male leopard plays no part in rearing the young, but the female is an attentive mother. She gives birth in some rocky crevice, carefully hidden from the large ground predators, but if she senses that a lion or a hyena has sniffed her out, she takes no risks and transports her cubs to some other hiding place. During the course of her territorial wanderings, she will have located, investigated and remembered all the possible crevices available to her and may move her cubs several times in quick succession, rather than adopt a defensive posture at the entrance to her den. Once again, caution rules. The cubs have a special response to being picked up

The leopard's powerful neck muscles allow it to carry heavy prey high into a tree.

by the scruff of the neck. Instead of struggling, they go completely limp. This is an inborn reaction, and human beings who have the task of hand-rearing abandoned cubs soon discover that they can exploit this reaction even with older, more boisterous cubs. Pick them up in your arms like a baby and they may struggle, writhe, scratch and even bite, but hold them up firmly by the scruff of the neck, and they cannot help subsiding into limp submission.

Without this reaction in the wild, the mother would find it hard to transport her offspring quickly to safety.

Perhaps surprisingly, there is no fixed breeding season. An adult female without a family will come onto heat for a few days every month until there is a successful mating. Gestation lasts for about 100 days. The typical leopard litter contains three cubs. Single cubs are known and there may be as many as six, but these extremes are rare. Born blind, the cubs' eyes open at six days. The mother will bring solid food to the den for them daily once they are about six weeks old and at the age of roughly four months they start to accompany her when she is out hunting. The cubs stay dependent on their mother for many months and will not fend for themselves until they are at least a year and a half. Some of them will stay around their mother even longer, until they are nearly two years old. They will become sexually mature by the time they are about two and a half years old. The mother will not mate again until all her cubs have left her. The mortality rate among leopard cubs is high. It has been estimated that, during their first year, 50 per cent of them will not survive. One third of these will be killed by predators such as hyenas and lions, and the rest will die of starvation.[2]

Adult leopards have three main facial expressions: relaxed, defensive and aggressive. In the relaxed face, the eyes are not widely staring, the nose skin is smooth and the ears are pointed about three-quarters forward. In the defensive expression, the eyes have a wide-open fixed stare, the nose is wrinkled and the mouth is open showing the large canine teeth. The ears may point directly forward or lie flat. This defensive expression is usually accompanied by hissing and snarling. The aggressive face – the expression of a leopard that is about to attack – displays fixed staring eyes, a smooth nose and the ears turned to show their backs. To most people, the defensive face of the leopard looks

The facial expressions of the leopard: left: defensive; below: ready to attack.

The melanistic leopard, often referred to as the black panther.

more frightening than the aggressive face. This is, of course, its function: to make the enemy recoil and move away when the leopard is cornered. But as far as the leopard's emotional state is concerned, this is not an out-and-out 'attack face', but the result of a mixture of fear and aggression. When a leopard is seriously aggressive and is about to make a leap at the enemy, or pounce on its prey, it holds a staring expression with its eyes and has its ears half-rotated.

The spotted coat of each leopard is unique, like a human fingerprint. Fieldworkers usually identify individual animals in the district they are studying by recording the pattern of the rows of 'whisker-spots' on the left and right cheeks. A 1991 research study made in Sri Lanka, using whisker-spot identification and involving 21 wild leopards, 'found that it was effective for distinguishing nineteen leopards with 95 per cent reliability, and 15 per cent with 99 per cent reliability'.[3] There is one colour variant of the leopard that used to be thought of as a separate species: the black panther. This is in reality an ordinary leopard carrying a recessive gene for melanism. Displaying an all-black coat has one advantage and one disadvantage. The advantage is that, in the dead of night, the predator becomes well-nigh invisible. The disadvantage is that in daylight, or even half-light, it becomes more conspicuous. Clearly, the disadvantage must outweigh the advantage, or the occurrence of black leopards would be much greater than it is. They are rare in most regions, but in the steamy hot jungles of the Malay peninsula they are much more frequent and, in some districts, they make up as much as 50 per cent of the wild leopard population.

12 Leopard Conservation

Like all large mammals in the wild, the leopard has suffered badly from the dramatic increase in the world's human population, robbing it of more and more of its natural habitat. Despite the fact that its geographical range is greater than that of any of the other big cats, and despite its cautious, secretive nature, its numbers worldwide have been seriously reduced in recent times. It has been reported that leopards have disappeared from almost 40 per cent of their traditional range in Africa, and from over 50 per cent of their range in Asia. They are now extinct in six of the countries that they used to occupy and their survival in six other countries is in doubt. The last time a leopard was recorded in North Africa, for example, was back in 2002; since then, nothing.

A century ago their dramatic fall in numbers across the globe was largely due to the popularity of leopard skins in the world of high fashion. As recently as the 1960s, up to 10,000 skins were imported annually into the United States to supply fashionable women eager to wear a leopard-skin coat. Then, in the 1970s, a ban was introduced, forbidding the importation of any such skins, and the fashion world began to adopt a new attitude towards the wearing of any kind of animal fur. Leopards were suddenly much safer from hunters' guns, but one great threat remained: the spread of human populations. In the 1960s, there were only 3,000 million people on earth; since then, this number has more than doubled. That increase has been greatest in developing countries, where the 3,000 million extra people have been pushing deeper and deeper into what was once the domain of wildlife. Leopards have lost their habitats and, in addition, have been shot or trapped because they became a threat to human life. In tropical cities, they have even been reduced to scavenging garbage bins at night, like mangy stray dogs.

What is the present assessment of the shrinking world of the leopard? How many are left, where are they safe and where are they most at risk? In addition to the global conservation societies such as the International Union for Conservation of Nature (IUCN), several specialist groups have been established

The present geographical range of the leopard, 2001.

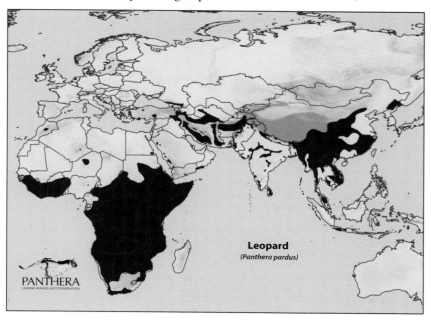

Leopard
(Panthera pardus)

PANTHERA
LEADERS IN WILD CAT CONSERVATION

to monitor the plight of wild leopards in the twenty-first century. In South Africa, the Leopard Conservation Project was established in 2000. With its headquarters in Johannesburg, it has the triple aim of protection, research and education. Its protection strategy has been to target poachers and trappers; its research has involved the fitting of cellphone collars to wild leopards to study their movements within their natural environment; and its educational efforts have been directed towards helping farmers to protect their livestock from leopard attacks. The South African research aims to increase knowledge of leopard population and territory sizes in specific regions, create photographic database of individuals, analyse prey preferences and investigate reproduction and mortality rates. Given the leopard's retiring nature, this is a daunting task, although it has been made slightly easier by the fact that loss of habitat has forced the leopard out into the open more frequently than in the past.

There are other leopard conservation projects active today in South Africa. In the east of the country, in the region now called KwaZulu Natal, the Munyawana Leopard Project is operating in the Phinda Game Reserve. Making use of radio-telemetry and camera-trap surveys, the conservationists in this region are compiling records of leopard mortality rates and finding, to their dismay, that these have doubled in recent times. One of the problems with protected game reserves here, and elsewhere, is that the wild occupants of the reserves do not recognize the boundaries of their safe homes. As soon as they stray outside, they are prey to human hunters and poachers.

A third leopard project in South Africa is centred on the huge Kruger National Park. The Greater Kruger Leopard Conservation Science Project was set up by the African Wildlife Foundation in the National Park to study the leopard populations there, their competition with other large carnivores, and their interactions with local people.

In the far north of the global range of the leopard, the rarest of all its subspecies, the Amur leopard, is on the brink of disappearing for ever as a wild animal. This magnificently thick-furred, cold-climate form once inhabited a wide area across northern China and parts of eastern Russia, but is now only managing to cling on in one small region of the Primorsky Krai in the far southeast corner of Russia. There, it has been reduced to a pathetically small wild population of no more than 35 animals. A combination of poaching, the deliberate setting of forest fires each spring and hunters killing the deer on which it relies for food has led to the bizarre situation that there are now at least three times as many

The rare Amur leopard.

Amur leopards in zoos as there are in the wild. Coordinated attempts are now being made to set up a game reserve north of Vladivostok, far away from human populations, where some of the zoo-bred leopards can be released to establish a new, wild population. The region selected for this experiment is one that used to be occupied by wild Amur leopards, so the habitat is natural for the species. London Zoo and Moscow Zoo are working together to achieve this goal, but it is fraught with difficulties, not least the repeated failure of well-meaning attempts with other species to reintroduce captive-bred animals into the wild. The young of wild animals that manage to mature from birth to adulthood learn so much about their environment that they are well equipped to survive its many hazards. They become jungle-wise in the same way that an urban child becomes streetwise. No matter how thoughtfully a zoo-bred leopard cub has been raised, it will always be at a disadvantage when placed in a wild habitat, even if that habitat is one that is completely natural to its species. So it remains to be seen whether this brave attempt to save the Amur leopard will succeed.

Finally, how many leopards are alive today in the entire world? One report gives the following figures as the highest assessments:

African leopard	25,000
Asian leopard	1,290
Sri Lankan leopard	950
Javan leopard	250
Arabian leopard	250
Amur leopard	35
LEOPARD TOTAL	27,775

These figures sound convincing until one reads another report that gives the total figure as 100,000. Yet another authority puts the figure as high as 262,000. The differences between these figures are so huge that the natural reaction is to trust none of them. Bearing in mind the secretive nature of the leopard, this mistrust is probably justified. Taking an accurate census of the number of wild leopards alive today is virtually impossible.

Timeline of the Leopard

2.6–5.3 MYA	470,000–825,000 YEARS AGO	170,000–300,000 YEARS AGO	23,000 YEARS AGO
Pliocene fossils of ancestral leopards found in England, France and Italy	Modern leopard evolved in Africa	Modern leopard spreads across Asia	Oldest known image of a leopard is found in the Chauvet Cave in France

1225–50	1616	1820	1828
In the bestiary known as Bodleian 764, the leopard is described as signifying 'either the Devil, full of a diversity of vices, or the sinner, spotted with crimes'	Rubens portrays the violent killing of a leopard in his painting *Tiger, Lion and Leopard Hunt*	Edward Hicks paints the first of 62 versions of *The Peaceable Kingdom* in which friendly leopards lie down with lambs	London Zoo receives its first leopard. By 1924 a total of 38 leopards will have been born at the zoo

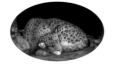

1935	1938	1948	1960s	1972
Edgar Rice Burroughs's book *Tarzan and the Leopard Men* appears and brings the African terror cult to the attention of a wide audience	Howard Hawks films his classic comedy about a tame leopard, *Bringing Up Baby*, starring Cary Grant and Katharine Hepburn	The reign of terror of the tribal cult of the leopard-men is finally brought to an end	Over 25,000 leopards are being killed annually to supply the fashion trade with fur coats	The USA bans any trade in leopards or leopard parts, heralding the collapse of the fashion for leopard-fur coats

6,000 YEARS AGO	1500 BC	AD 80–AD 523	9TH CENTURY

Plaster relief of a pair of leopards found at the ancient town of Catal Huyuk in Turkey

A tame leopard on a collar and lead is shown in an ancient Egyptian tomb painting

Countless leopards are slaughtered in the arena for the amusement of the Roman throng, including 410 during the opening celebrations of the Coliseum

Bronze leopard on conch-shaped vase from Igbo-Ukwu, West Africa

1839	1897	1909	1926

Queen Victoria commissions Edwin Landseer to paint a portrait of Isaac Van Amburgh with his trained leopards, after enjoying his performance

A pair of ivory leopard figures is looted from Benin City in West Africa and presented to Queen Victoria

The leopard is classified as vermin by the British colonial government in East Africa because it attacks livestock. Unlimited hunting of leopard is permitted

The man-eating leopard of Rudraprayag is shot by Jim Corbett

1982	2000	2001	2011

The American sport-hunting lobby gains permission for the export and import of leopard trophies obtained in sub-Saharan Africa, although commercial trade in leopards remains banned

The Leopard Conservation Project is established in South Africa, with its headquarters in Johannesburg

The annual quota of African leopards approved for export when shot by sport-hunters is 2,345, although only 741 are taken

A film record is made of a leopard attacking a forestry official in West Bengal, one of many recent incursions of leopards into human habitations in India

Appendix 1: Classification

LEOPARD SPECIES

Panthera pardus (Linnaeus, 1758)

LEOPARD SUBSPECIES

The nine subspecies recognized by the IUCN are shown below along
with their geographical range:

African leopard (*P. p. pardus*, Linnaeus, 1758)	sub-Saharan Africa
Indian leopard (*P. p. fusca*, Meyer, 1794)	Indian subcontinent
Javan leopard (*P. p. melas*, Cuvier, 1809)	Java, Indonesia
Arabian leopard (*P. p. nimr*, Hemprich and Ehrenberg, 1833)	Arabian peninsula
Amur leopard (*P. p. orientalis*, Schlegel, 1857)	Russian Far East, Korean peninsula and northeast China
North Chinese leopard (*P. p. japonensis*, Gray, 1862)	northern China

Caucasian leopard	central Asia: the Caucasus,
(*P. p. ciscaucasica*, Satunin, 1914),	Turkmenistan and
later described as Persian leopard	northern Iran
(*P. p. saxicolor*, Pocock, 1927)	

Indochinese leopard   mainland Southeast Asia
(*P. p. delacouri*, Pocock, 1930)

Sri Lankan leopard   Sri Lanka
(*P. p. kotiya*, Deraniyagala, 1956)

A morphological analysis of characters of leopard skulls implies the validity of two more subspecies:

Anatolian leopard   western Turkey
(*P. p. tulliana*, Valenciennes, 1856)

Balochistan leopard   Pakistan, and possibly also
(*P. p. sindica*, Pocock, 1930)   parts of Afghanistan and Iran

HYBRID LEOPARDS

A number of leopard hybrids have been bred in captivity, as follows:

     leopon (male leopard x female lion)
     lipard (male lion x female leopard)
     jagupard (male jaguar x female leopard)
     leguar (male leopard x female jaguar)
     pumapard (male puma x female leopard) (shows dwarfism)

Appendix 2: Other Leopards

This is a book about the common leopard, *Panthera pardus*, but there are four other species that have been given the name of leopard in the past. It is beyond the scope of this volume to deal with them in any detail, but each deserves a brief mention. They are:

SNOW LEOPARD (*UNCIA UNCIA*)

Snow leopards inhabit cold, rocky mountainous regions in central Asia and differ from the other big cats in that they cannot roar. They are found in the Himalayas, Altai, Tien Shan and Karakoram Mountains. Compared with the common leopard, the Snow leopard has a small head and small, rounded ears, but its feet are huge and have fur underneath that acts as a kind of protective 'snowshoe' on the frozen ground. It is a rare animal today, with only about 6,000 left in the wild.

HUNTING LEOPARD (*ACINONYX JUBATUS*)

In colonial times, this species was referred to as the hunting leopard because it was so often domesticated and employed as a hunting aid. In sixteenth-century India, for example, the great Moghul emperor Akbar, during his 49-year reign, owned the astonishing total of 9,000 trained hunting leopards. These were employed to chase down gazelle and blackbuck on his spectacular royal hunts. Since then, it has become

The Snow leopard
(*Uncia uncia*).

better known by its Hindi name of cheetah, to avoid confusion with the true leopard. In 1781, the first publication to mention its new name referred to the animal as 'The Hunting Leopard, or Indian Chittah'. Even as late as 1899, the word 'cheetah' was still being referred to as 'the native name of the hunting-leopard of India', but today its use has become universal.

The cheetah has been described as a leopard that wanted to be a greyhound. The fastest of all land mammals, it can reach a top speed of 101 kph (63 mph) and some claim that it has managed 120 kph (75 mph). Its slender, streamlined body is adapted for hunting over flat, open country, where it can overtake its prey in a non-stop sprint. Like a sports car, it can accelerate from 0 to 100 kph in five seconds. Once it has caught up with its quarry, the cheetah knocks it over and applies a throat bite that chokes the animal to death. Uniquely among the members of the cat family, it has sacrificed the special advantage of having sharp, retractile claws, a modification to its feet that make them that little bit faster. Its markings differ from those of the leopard, its solid, round spots contrasting with the hollow rosettes of its heavier relative. This difference is useful when trying to identify the exact species depicted in early illustrations.

The Hunting leopard (*Acinonyx jubatus*).

There is an extremely rare mutation of the cheetah called the King cheetah, which has a unique fur pattern. Of the few that have been recorded, nearly all have come from the southeast region of Africa.

At the beginning of the twentieth century, there were over 100,000 cheetahs in the world, but by the end of the century the number had dwindled to no more than 10,000, the once huge range of the cheetah having been dramatically reduced. Today, it is found only in Africa, with the exception of a small population of about 50 to 100 animals still surviving in a remote corner of Iran. The once plentiful population of Indian cheetahs was totally exterminated by trophy hunters and other

The King cheetah.

forms of human interference during the twentieth century. The last three Asiatic cheetahs were shot by the Maharajah of Surguja in 1947.

AMERICAN LEOPARD (*PANTHERA ONCA*)

Like the cheetah, the American leopard, or American panther as it was known, has been given its local name of jaguar to avoid confusion with the true leopard. The name is a Portuguese corruption of the Brazilian name, taken from the language of the coastal Tupi people who were cannibal tribes that were largely exterminated by the Europeans.

At first glance the jaguar is very similar to the leopard, but it has a slightly heavier build and there are small, black spots inside its rosette markings. These interior spots are never seen on the coat of a leopard. As with all big cats, its range has been reduced by human interference. The last United States jaguars disappeared in the early 1960s and it is now extinct in North America. It is managing to hold on in the forests of Central America and tropical South America, but its estimated world population is now down to fewer than 10,000 animals.

Its way of life is similar to that of the leopard. Its diet consists mostly of peccaries and large rodents such as the capybara and the coypu.

The American leopard (*Panthera onca*).

The Clouded
leopard (*Neofelis
nebulosa*).

The Clouded leopard (*Neofelis nebulosa*).

Unlike the leopard, it enjoys hunting in the water and otters and various fish are included in its diet.

In the mythology of the indigenous peoples of Central and South America, the jaguar played an important role. For the Aztecs, it was a spirit animal with magical powers and for the Mayas, it was a god of the underworld.

CLOUDED LEOPARD (*NEOFELIS NEBULOSA*)

The Clouded leopards of the forests of tropical Asia are intermediate between the big cats and the small cats. They are not closely related to the true leopards but do share the habit of dragging their kill up into trees. They have been described as the best tree-climbers in the entire cat family. Their acrobatic skills among the branches are extraordinary. These leopards can hang down from a branch while clinging on with their hind legs, and they can walk along a horizontal branch while upside down. They can also climb down a vertical tree trunk head first. Anatomically, they are unusual in having exceptionally long canine teeth, and it is because of which Clouded leopards have sometimes been referred to as the modern-day sabre-tooths. The spots on their coats are so big that they have joined up to create a reticulated pattern similar to that seen on some giraffes.

The global population of wild Clouded leopards is estimated to have fallen below the 10,000 mark in recent years. In addition, it is said that there are about 200 of them in zoos worldwide at the present time. The beauty of their coat has led to widespread trapping and hunting in certain regions. A recent study of four markets in Burma revealed the presence of no fewer than 279 Clouded leopard skins, despite the fact that the species is officially protected in that country. It takes 25 pelts to make a single Clouded leopard coat and these remain popular in parts of the Far East, regardless of recent changes in attitude, towards the wearing of fur.

SUNDA CLOUDED LEOPARD (*NEOFELIS DIARDI*)

In 2006, the Sunda clouded leopard of Borneo and Sumatra was distinguished as a separate species from the mainland Asian clouded leopard. Although it has been proved that the two species are genetically distinct and that their populations have been separated from one another for

The Sunda clouded leopard (*Neofelis diardi*), from William Jardine, *The Natural History of the Felinae* (Edinburgh, 1837).

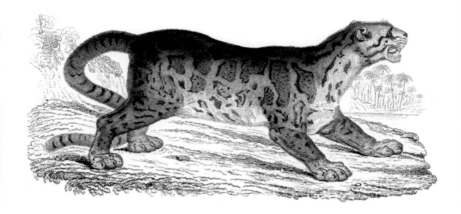

159

1.4 million years, they remain very similar in appearance. One of the few visible differences is that the Sunda clouded leopard has more spotted ovals than the Asian clouded leopard. As part of its adaptation to arboreal living, the Sunda clouded leopard has hind legs that are longer than its front legs and, like the Asian clouded leopard, it can climb down trees head first. On Borneo it spends more of its time on the ground, compared with its counterpart on Sumatra. This is thought to be because of greater predatory competition at ground level on Sumatra.

Extensive logging on Borneo and Sumatra will, if it continues at its present rate, cause the Sunda clouded leopard to become extinct by the end of the present century. Over 10 per cent of the lowland forest has been lost in the past ten years and there is no sign of this abating. When the locals in Borneo show you great swathes of felled forest, they do so not with shame but with pride. They are emulating what the respected Europeans did to their own countries in the past and see it as progress rather that desecration. Their wild felines are going to need all the help they can get.

Appendix 3: Filmography

1909 *Leopard Hunting in Abyssinia*, directed by Roberto Omegna (documentary)

1920 *The Leopard Woman*, directed by Wesley Ruggles (silent drama), starring Louise Glaum

1928 *The Leopard Lady*, directed by Rupert Julian (drama), starring Jacqueline Logan

1938 *Bringing up Baby*, directed by Howard Hawks (comedy), starring Cary Grant and Katharine Hepburn.

1940 *Leopard Men of Africa*, directed by Allyn Butterfield (drama)

1942 *Cat People*, directed by Jacques Tourneur (drama), starring Simone Simon

1943 *The Leopard Man*, directed by Jacques Tourneur (drama)

1946 *Tarzan and the Leopard Woman*, directed by Kurt Neumann (drama), starring Johnny Weismuller

1954 *Killer Leopard*, directed by Ford Beebe (drama), starring Johnny Sheffield

1955 *The Leopard Men: Sheena, Queen of the Jungle*, directed by Stuart Gilmore (TV drama), starring Irish McCalla

1958 *Killer Leopard*, directed by Joseph Sterling (TV drama), starring Rhodes Reason

1963 *The Leopard*, directed by Luchino Visconti (drama), starring Burt Lancaster

1966 *Leopard on the Loose*, directed by Paul Stanley (TV drama), starring Ron Ely

2006 *The Eye of the Leopard*, directed by Beverly and Dereck Joubert (TV documentary), narrated by Jeremy Irons

2007 *Stalking Leopards*, directed by Eric Millot (TV documentary), narrated by Simon Barritt

2008 *Leopard Attack*, directed by Steve Klayman (TV documentary), starring Scott Lope

2009 *Man-eating Leopards*, directed by Matt Thompson (TV documentary), starring Austin Stevens

2010 *Leopards*, directed by Richard Graveling (TV documentary), starring Ray Mears

2010 *Revealing the Leopard*, directed by Nigel Cole (TV documentary), narrated by Jim Conrad

2010 *Stalking the Leopard* (National Geographic TV documentary), narrated by Keith David

2010 *The Secret Leopards* (TV documentary), narrated by Jonathan Scott

References

1 ANCIENT LEOPARDS

1 Jean-Marie Chauvet et al., *Chauvet Cave, The Discovery of the World's Oldest Paintings* (London, 1996), p. 34; Jean Clottes, *Return to Chauvet Cave. Excavating the Birthplace of Art: The First Full Report* (London, 2003), pp. 77–9.
2 James Mellaart, *Catal Huyuk* (London, 1967).
3 Sonia Cole, in A. Houghton Broderick, ed., *Animals in Archaeology* (London, 1972).
4 Arielle P. Kozloff, *Animals in Ancient Art* (Cleveland, OH, 1981).
5 Patrick F. Houlihan, *The Animal World of the Pharaohs* (London, 1996).
6 Jocelyn Toynbee, *Animals in Roman Life and Art* (London, 1973), pp. 82–6.

2 TRIBAL LEOPARDS

1 Jessica Rawson, *Animals in Art* (London, 1977).
2 Barbara Plankensteiner, *Visions of Africa – Benin* (Milan, 2010), p. 114.
3 Justin Cordwell, in William A. Fagaly, ed., *Ancestors of Congo Square: African Art in the New Orleans Museum of Art* (London, 2011).
4 Jan Vansina, *Art History in Africa: An Introduction to Method* (London, 1984), p. 63.
5 Judith Gleason ed., *Leaf and Bone: African Praise Poems* (New York, 1994), p. 129.

3 LEOPARD CULTS

1 David Pratten, *The Man-Leopard Murders: History and Society in Colonial Nigeria* (Edinburgh, 2007).
2 Edgar Rice Burroughs, *Tarzan and the Leopard Men* (Tarzana, CA, 1935).

4 LEOPARD HUNTING

1 Theodore Roosevelt, *African Game Trails* (New York, 1910).
2 Brian Herne, *White Hunters: The Golden Age of African Safaris* (New York, 1999).
3 Eva Stuart-Watts, *Africa's Dome of Mystery* (London, 1930).
4 Lou Hallamore and Bruce Woods, *CHUI! A Guide to Hunting the African Leopard*, 2nd edn (Agoura, CA, 2011).
5 Guy Balme and Luke Hunter, 'The Leopard: The World's Most Persecuted Big Cat', *Conservation in Action, Twelfth Vision Annual*, www.panthera.org, pp. 88–94.
6 Shuja Islam and Zohra Islam, *Hunting Dangerous Game with the Maharajas in the Indian Sub-Continent* (New Dehli, 2004).
7 'Endangered Leopards Battling for Survival', *Times of India* (18 May 2010).

5 LEOPARD ATTACKS

1 Charles Kimberlin Brain, *The Hunters or the Hunted?* (Chicago, 1981), fig. 221; Simon J. M. Davis, *The Archaeology of Animals* (London, 1987), p. 92; K. Zuberbühler and D. Jenny, 'Leopard Predation and Primate Evolution', *Journal of Human Evolution*, XLIII/6 (2002), pp. 873–86.
2 J. C. Daniel (1927–2011), former curator of the Bombay Natural History Society, describes man-eating leopards in his book, *The Leopard in India: A Natural History* (Dehradun, India, 2009).
3 Jim Corbett, *The Man-eating Leopard of Rudraprayag* (Oxford, 1947).

4 'Leopards, 21st-century Cats', television documentary by Ron Whitaker, shown on BBC2 on 17 May 2013 as a *Natural World* special.

5 Maitland Edey, *The Cats of Africa* (New York, 1968), p. 96.

8 LEOPARDS IN ART

1 T. H. White, *The Book of Beasts* (London, 1954), p. 14, this being a translation of a twelfth-century bestiary housed in the Cambridge University Library, numbered II.4.26.

2 Ibid., p. 17.

3 Pliny the Elder, *Natural History*, Book 8, 23 (1st century AD).

4 Ann Payne, *Medieval Beasts* (London, 1990).

5 Sotheby's New York, 22 May 2008, Lot 60. Edward Hicks *The Peaceable Kingdom with the Leopard of Serenity*, 1846–8, sold for $9,673,000.

9 CIRCUS LEOPARDS

1 Cicero, *Letters to Friends*, trans. D. R. Shackleton Bailey (Cambridge, MA, 2001).

2 Michèle Blanchard-Lemée, Mongi Ennaïfer, Hédi Slim and Latifa Slim, *Mosaics of Roman Africa* (London, 1996).

3 Johann Georg Graevius, *Thesaurus antiquitatum Romanorum* (1694–9).

10 TAME LEOPARDS

1 Michaela Denis, *Leopard in my Lap* (London, 1955).

2 Arjan Singh, *Prince of Cats* (London, 1982).

3 Sylvie Robert, *Tippi: My Book of Africa* (Capetown, 2005).

11 WILD LEOPARDS

1 Edward Topsell, *The History of Four-footed Beasts* (London, 1658), pp. 447–55.

2 Andrew Kitchener, *The Natural History of the Wild Cats*
   (London, 1991), p. 210.
3 Sriyanie Miththapala, 'How to tell a Leopard by its Spots',
   in *Great Cats*, ed. John Seidenstucker and Susan Lumpkin
   (London, 1991), p. 112.

Select Bibliography

Adamson, Joy, *Queen of Shaba: The Story of an African Leopard* (London, 1980)

Alderton, David, *Wild Cats of the World* (London, 1993)

Aldrovandi, Ulyssis, *Opera omnia, de quadrupedibus digitatis* (Bologna, 1645)

Badino, Guido, *Big Cats of the World* (London, 1975)

Bailey, Theodore, *The African Leopard* (New York, 1993)

Barber, Richard, *Bestiary* (Woodbridge, 1993)

Beatty, Kenneth James, *Human Leopards* (London, 1915)

Benton, Janetta Rebold, *The Medieval Menagerie* (New York, 1992)

Bindloss, Harold, *The League of the Leopard* (London, 1904)

Broderick, A. Houghton, *Animals in Archaeology* (London, 1972)

Burroughs, Edgar Rice, *Tarzan and the Leopard Men* (Tarzana, CA, 1935) (novel)

Chauvet, Jean-Marie et al., *Chauvet Cave: The Discovery of the World's Oldest Paintings* (London, 1996)

Clottes, Jean, *Return to Chauvet Cave. Excavating the Birthplace of Art: The First Full Report* (London, 2003)

Corbett, Jim, *The Man-eating Leopard of Rudraprayag* (Oxford, 1947)

Court, Alfred, *My Life with the Big Cats* (New York, 1955)

Daniel, J. C., *The Leopard in India: A Natural History* (Dehradun, India, 2009)

Denis, Armand, *Cats of the World* (London, 1964)

Denis, Michaela, *Leopard in my Lap* (London, 1955)

Dixon, Franklin W., *The Search for the Snow Leopard* (London, 1996)

Edey, Maitland A., *The Cats of Africa* (New York, 1968)

Gaunt, Mary, *The Arms of the Leopard* (London, 1923) (novel)

Gesner, Konrad, *Historia Animalaia, Icones Animalium Quadrupedum* (Zurich, 1560)

Green, Richard, *Wild Cat Species of the World* (Plymouth, 1991)

Guggisberg, C.A.W., *Wild Cats of the World* (London, 1975)

Guillot, René, *Michel Fodai and the Leopard-Men*, trans Joan Selby-Lowndes (London, 1969) (novel)

Herne, Brian, *White Hunters: The Golden Age of African Safaris* (New York, 1999)

Houlihan, Patrick F., *The Animal World of the Pharaohs* (London, 1996)

Islam, Shuja and Zohra Islam, *Hunting Dangerous Game with the Maharajas in the Indian Sub-Continent* (New Dehli, 2004)

Jennison, George, *Animals for Show and Pleasure in Ancient Rome* (Manchester, 1937)

Jonstonnus, Johannes, *Historiae Naturalis* (Amsterdam, 1657)

Jordan, Bill, *Leopard: Habits, Life Cycle, Food Chain, Threats* (Orlando, 2001)

Kennerley, Juba, *The Terror of the Leopard Men* (New York, 1951)

Kitchener, Andrew, *The Natural History of the Wild Cats* (London, 1991)

Kozloff, Arielle P., *Animals in Ancient Art* (Cleveland, OH, 1981)

Lampedusa, Guiseppi Tomasi di, *The Leopard* (London, 1960)

Leiris, Michel and Jacqueline Delange, *African Art* (London, 1968)

Lindskog, Birger, *African Leopard Men* (Uppsala, 1954)

Lloyd, Joan Barclay, *African Animals in Renaissance Literature and Art* (Oxford, 1971)

Matthessen, Peter, *The Snow Leopard* (London, 1989)

May, Earl Chapin, *The Circus from Rome to Ringling* (New York, 1932)

Mellaart, James, *Catal Huyuk* (London, 1967)

Payne, Ann, *Medieval Beasts* (London, 1990)

Perry, Richard, *The World of the Jaguar* (Newton Abbot, 1970)

Pratten, David, *The Man-Leopard Murders: History and Society in Colonial Nigeria* (Edinburgh, 2007)

Rabinowitz, Alan, *Jaguar* (London, 1987)

Rawson, Jessica, *Animals in Art* (London, 1977)

Robert, Sylvie, *Tippi: My Book of Africa* (Capetown, 2005)

Roosevelt, Theodore, *African Game Trails* (New York, 1910)

Schaller, George, *Golden Shadows, Flying Hooves* (London, 1974)

Scott, Jonathan, *The Leopard's Tale* (London, 1985)

Scott, Jonathan and Angela Scott, *Big Cat Diary: Leopard* (London, 2003)

Seidenstucker, John and Susan Lumpkin, eds, *Great Cats* (London, 1991)

Shaw, James, *The Leopard Men* (London, 1953) (novel)

Singh, Arjan, *Prince of Cats* (London, 1982)

Topsell, Edward, *The History of Four-footed Beasts and Serpents* (London, 1658)

Toynbee, Jocelyn, *Animals in Roman Life and Art* (London, 1973)

Turnbull-Kemp, Peter, *The Leopard* (Cape Town, 1967)

Van Riel, Fransje, *My Life with Leopards* (Johannesburg, 2012)

West, Paul, *The Snow Leopard* (New York, 1965)

White, Stewart Edward, *The Leopard Woman* (London, 1915) (novel)

White, T. H., *The Book of Beasts* (London, 1954)

Associations and Websites

THE AMUR LEOPARD AND TIGER ALLIANCE
alta@zsl.org
The Zoological Society of London and several other conservation
agencies are coordinating a rescue operation for the nearly extinct
Amur leopard.

THE BOTSWANA PREDATOR CONSERVATION TRUST
www.bpctrust.org
This was set up in 1989 to investigate African wild dogs
and to preserve their habitat, but then expanded to include
Africa's other major carnivore predators, including the leopard.
Most of its research is focused on the important Okavango
Delta region.

THE GREATER KRUGER LEOPARD CONSERVATION SCIENCE PROJECT
www.awf.org
A project set up by the African Wildlife Foundation in the
Kruger National Park to study the leopard populations there,
their competition with other large carnivores and their
interactions with local people. The AWF is one of the oldest
of all conservation societies, having had its beginnings as
far back as 1961, when the concept of animal conservation
was in its infancy.

THE LEOPARD CONSERVATION PROJECT

www.leopardcon.co.za

Based in Johannesburg, the project aims to protect the South African leopard, to carry out research into its ecology and to educate local people about coexisting with leopards. It was founded in 2000.

THE MYNYAWANA LEOPARD PROJECT

www.panthera.org

A project set up on the east coast of South Africa, centred on the Phinda Game Reserve to study mortality rates among the local leopards, using modern, high-tech equipment. This project is one of the many feline conservation activities of PANTHERA, founded by Dr Thomas Kaplan in 2006.

WILDLIFE CONSERVATION SOCIETY INDIA

www.wcsindia.org

Wildlife Conservation Society India is a national organization registered in 2011. There are over 600 nature reserves in the country, which cover about 5 per cent of the land. However, human population growth poses serious conservation challenges. Effective action to save wildlife and wild places is now an urgent need. WCS India supports a multi-pronged conservation strategy that includes cutting-edge wildlife research, context-specific conservation models and passionate local interventions. They combine long-term collaborations with local communities to resolve conflicts and reduce their impact on wildlife.

Photo Acknowledgements

The author and publishers wish to express their thanks to the below sources of illustrative material and/or permission to reproduce it. Some locations are also given in the captions for the sake of brevity.

Photo AIMare: p. 26; © AP / Manas Paran, *The Sunday Indian* / PA Images: p. 61; courtesy of Ardmore Ceramic Art: p. 84; photo © Yann Arthus-Bertrand / Corbis: p. 72; collection of the author: p. 109; photos courtesy of the author: pp. 9, 10, 109, 133, 156 (top); photo Salil Bera: p. 60; Berlin State Museum: p. 37 (top right); Bibliothèque Municipale, Cambrai: p. 94; photo BigStock dmitrii_designer: p. 81 (foot); photos © Tom Brakefield / Corbis: pp. 156 (foot), 158; British Library, London (photo © The British Library): p. 92; British Museum, London: pp. 30, 33; Brooklyn Museum, New York: p. 103; from Edgar Rice Burroughs, *Tarzan and the Leopard Men* (Tarzana, California, 1935): p. 43; photo courtesy Bwoom-Gallery, Wolfenbüttel / www.bwoom-gallery.com: p. 35; Cappella dei Magi, Palazzo Medici-Riccardi, Florence: p. 95; photos Caters News Agency: pp. 60, 137, 138; photo W. A. Conduitt: p. 58; from Jim Corbett, *The Man-Eating Leopard of Rudraprayag* (London, 1948): p. 59; photo courtesy Dimondstein Tribal Arts: p. 38; photo © DLILLC / Corbis: p. 157; photo John Dominis – Time & Life Pictures / Getty Images): p. 136; photo © Michael Durham / Minden Pictures / Corbis: p. 141 (top); Egyptian Museum, Cairo: p. 21; Egyptian Museum, Turin: p. 20; from *The Encyclopædia Britannica; or a Dictionary of Arts and Sciences compiled upon a new plan . . .* (Edinburgh, 1771): p. 9; courtesy of the artist (Walton Ford) and Paul Kasmin Gallery:

Index